Celtic Journeys

Shirley Toulson is a poet, educationist and travel writer. Among her published books are The Drovers Roads of Wales, The Celtic Alternative *and* The Celtic Year.

Celtic Journeys

in Scotland and the North of England

✠

Shirley Toulson

Maps drawn by John Gilkes

Fount
An Imprint of HarperCollinsPublishers

Fount Paperbacks is an Imprint of
HarperCollins*Religious*
Part of HarperCollins*Publishers*
77–85 Fulham Palace Road, London W6 8JB

First published in Great Britain in 1985 by Hutchinson & Co. (Publishers) Ltd
Published in 1995 by Fount Paperbacks

1   3   5   7   9   10   8   6   4   2

Copyright in the text and illustrations © 1985 Shirley Toulson
Copyright in the maps © 1995 John Gilkes

Shirley Toulson and John Gilkes assert the moral right to be
identified as the author and mapmaker of this work

A catalogue record for this book is
available from the British Library

ISBN 0 00 627882-5

Printed and bound in Great Britain by
HarperCollinsManufacturing Glasgow

Contents

Acknowledgements

It would have been impossible to produce this book without the help of the many people in different parts of Scotland and the north of England who gave up their time to talk to me about the traditions of the saints in their localities. I should like to use this opportunity to express my thanks for their generosity and patience, and to mention in particular the kindness of the Reverend Robin and Mrs Nancy Jones and Mrs Violet Harris of Mungrisdale in Cumbria; Mr William Barron, the curator of the museum at Whithorn, Galloway; Miss Marian Campbell, Mrs Anne M. Kahane and the Reverend H. R. Rogers of Kintyre; Mrs Kathleen Campbell of Oban; Mrs Jessie Young of Onich; Ian Galloway, warden of the Iona Community; Miss Beryl Alcorn of Kiltarlity; Mrs Katharine Stewart of Arbriachan; Mrs Loraine Maclean of Glen Urquhart; Mr Archie McKerracher of Dunblane; the Reverend D. S. A. Grieve of Arbirlot; Mr Gerald Bonner of the University of Durham; the Reverend Tony Duncan of Warksworth; the Reverend John Lyall, Mrs Helen Russell and Mrs Tina Docherty of Kingussie; Major General and Mrs R. Younger of Ravenswood, Old Melrose; and Mrs Audrey Fforde of Loch Tay. I alone am responsible for any factual errors in this text or for any misinterpretation of the information which these people gave me.

Chronology

635	Corman returns to Iona. Aidan arrives in Northumbria
664	Synod of Whitby. Birth of Bede at Jarrow
673	Council of Hereford declares British Church to be non-Catholic
675	Cuthbert retires to Inner Farne
679	Adomnan, Columba's biographer, becomes abbot of Iona
685	Cuthbert made bishop of Lindisfarne
687	20 March: death of Cuthbert
706	Nectan becomes king of the Picts. Strikes at Celtic Church
793	Danes invade Lindisfarne
801–5	Viking raids on Iona
1017	Cuthbert's body laid in the Saxon cathedral at Durham
1093	Present Durham Cathedral begun
1104	Cuthbert's body moved to its present position
1539	December: spoliation of Cuthbert's shrine at Durham by Henry VIII

Peregrinati – *the Wanderers*

The story of Celtic Christianity in the north begins with the Roman walls and the legions who manned them. The year is AD 133 and Hadrian's great stone-built wall, ten feet thick in many places, spans the neck of Britain from the Tyne to the Solway Firth. To the south the land flourishes under the administration of the Pax Romana, and even to the north the Belgians and Germans who man the wall make their presence felt, and have done ever since Agricola's victory over the Picts at Mons Graupius (somewhere near the Moray Firth) in AD 84.

Before Hadrian's Wall was five years old, a second, lesser wall was started to consolidate the Roman position in the north. Made of turf resting on rubble, the earthwork of Antoninus Pius's Wall stretched for thirty-seven miles from the Firth of Forth to Old Kilpatrick on the Clyde. It was occupied continuously to AD 145 and then spasmodically for another forty years. Between the greater and the lesser walls lay the district of Valentia, land that was to be uneasy border country for centuries. Here the first Celtic Christians spread the news of that other borderland between time and eternity.

The soldiers who manned the walls were free to follow any religion they chose, with two important exceptions. They were forbidden to subscribe to the rites of the native Druid culture of the conquered northerners; and they were not allowed to hold the Christian beliefs that had been brought up from the shores of the Mediterranean. The ban emphasizes the power of both creeds to disrupt a Roman soldier's prime allegiance to his state.

Even though he was a forbidden god, the legions brought news of Christ with them. Early in the third century, Tertullian of Carthage and Origen of Alexandria were both commenting on the spread of Christianity in Britain; and by 313, when Constantine's Edict of Milan finally recognized that faith as the official religion of Rome, the law, as usual, was simply catching up with events.

Druidism

Two strands come together to form the pattern of early Christianity in Britain: the Druidism on which it was planted and the practices of the Desert Fathers which inspired its asceticism. The Celtic Church was to take on many of the rites and traditions of the Druids. The saints whose journeys we are about to follow through northern Britain wore the spiritual mantles of the Druidic 'soul friends' who counselled and guided the leaders of the Iron Age tribes. Every monk had his 'soul friend', who guided his spiritual life without acting as any sort of intermediary between him and Christ.

Although the 'soul friend' did not possess the supernatural power of a priestly confessor, who can pronounce absolution and atonement, he was a beloved teacher. Human warmth is the quality, above all others, that the early saints possessed. Their hagiographers vie with each other in the tales they tell of the way their chosen subject could bend nature to suit his purposes, but in each case it is the kindliness of the man, and the affection he engendered, that lights the story of his life.

In many ways the miracles that were attributed to the historical saints match the exploits of the eternal beings of myth and the heroes of legend. Often their stories intertwine, grounding at special spots on the earth's surface. St Michael the Archangel is so linked, not with any earthly saint but with the Celtic deity Mannanàn Machêr, whose name is enshrined in the Isle of Man. As god of the sea he took the souls of the dead across the ocean to Paradise, leading them from this world to the next. So it is natural to find dedications to Michael by the sea shore and on high hills.

Although she belongs properly to Ireland, Bridget, Mary of the Gael, triple goddess of the Celts whose attributes cling to the sixth-century abbess of Kildare, has a firm hold on the Western Highlands as many a Kilbride placename proves. By tradition the Christian Bridget was the daughter of a Druid, and one Gaelic verse collected from South Uist names her father as Dugall the Brown and gives her genealogy for several generations, promising protection from bodily and spiritual ills to anyone who recites her line of descent as a charm.

The legendary Arthur and his Druid Merlin (whose home was in the Caledonian Forest) are as potent as the archangel and the goddess–nun in many of the stories that have grown up around the early saints. Galloway, Cumbria, Northumberland and the Borders abound with places in which some exploit of the hero-king has been celebrated. One legend even claims Kentigern's grandmother for Arthur's sister; and as the battles that the historical Arthur, or his prototype, fought took place during Christian lifetimes, it is surprising that there are not even more stories bringing saints and knights together.

Such stories as we have were originally sung by the bards. The poets in the Celtic hierarchy came only a little lower than the Druids, and most of the stories that have come down to us are attributed to the legendary Ossian, a bard who is supposed to have sung in the fourth century, although his poems were not collected in manuscript until a thousand years later.

The hagiographers who produced the lives of the northern saints were at work long before that. It is surprising how often the traditional tales that they worked from involved a beheading. Over and over again a missionary saint arriving (usually from across the water) at the place where he wished to make his first settlement would have his head cut off by the hostile inhabitants. So the first test of his supernatural powers was to restore his head to his body.

These absurd tales have a serious source. They spring from the Celtic reverence for the head as the abode of the soul and from their use of the symbol of headlessness to signify eternal life. So we have a non-fatal beheading in the Arthurian story of Gawain and the Green Knight; and it is fitting that the saints too, in the story at least, should provide the people with a similar token of eternity.

The Desert Fathers

So in stories at any rate the fables of pagan Druidism and the legends of the Christian court of King Arthur combine to form a tradition which harmonizes with the miracles, if not the teaching, of the saints. For that, and for the way the first Christian settlements were ordered, we must look to Egypt and the way of life exemplified by Anthony, Paul and Jerome. Many scholars have found a close affinity between the Celtic monasteries and that founded by St Anthony in Pispir in the third century, and by St John Cassian at Apt to the north of Marseilles two hundred years later, abut 420. The connection between the Celtic saints and the Eastern Christian tradition has continued for a long time; it is remarkable how the early saints of Britain, largely forgotten in their own country, are revered by members of the Orthodox Church.

Influenced by the Eastern practices, the first Christian communities in northern Britain arranged their settlements in such a manner that they were able to live their individual lives in separate cells, even though they belonged to a closely knit community. A certain amount of isolation was actively encouraged. Any man who professed any spiritual authority had to live out some of his days as a hermit, taking a retreat from the brotherhood and staying alone on an island or in a cave. These retreats were generally made during the Lents that led up to Christmas and Easter.

The work of these early monasteries, which took the form of a cluster of beehive huts around a central oratory, was officially divided into three parts: solitary prayer and worship; scholarship, which included the transcribing of the Scriptures; and active work for the community and for the general relief of sickness and distress. To these three aspects of a devout life in the Dark Ages, we must add a fourth: the need to wander, to give up the comparative comfort and security of a settled base and 'to journey for God'.

This journeying was more than a missionary expedition, for although the wandering Celtic Christians naturally told of their beliefs as they went from place to place, evangelizing was not their main concern. Their purpose was to walk for God, to enter the 'white martyrdom' of exile from home; and to follow Christ's injunctions to journey unimpeded by worldly possessions. They were also following the instincts of their own blood, for the Celts are inveterate travellers and adventurers. For although we may trust the sixth-century monk Gildas who called these early Christians 'Pilgrims for God' to whom it was not so much a weariness as a delight 'to voyage over the sea and to pace over broad tracts of land' (*De Excido*), the seventeenth-century writer Thomas Fuller was also just in his observation that most of the Celtic saints 'seem born under a travelling planet'.

The journeys that I follow in this book start with those of Ninian in the second half of the fourth century; by which time British Christianity had already managed to fall away from the purity of its beginnings, when Nelior, bishop of Carlisle, and Nicholas, bishop of Penrhyn, near modern Glasgow, were martyred under the Diocletian persecutions of the late third century.

Patrick, a near contemporary of Ninian, is the best-known saint of the north. Grandson of a priest and son of a Christian deacon, he is believed to have been born in 373 at the western end of the Antonine Wall. Although the date of his birth is uncertain, we know that he was at the height of his powers in the first half of the fifth century when he wrote about the decadence of the Church. He accused his fellow believers of having 'gone back from God', complaining that they 'had not kept His commandments, and were not obedient to our priests who used to warn us for our salvation'.

Patrick's missionary journeys belong to Ireland where he was taken by pirates as a young man; but we can find dedications to him in Cumbria, both in the tiny village of Bampton and at Patterdale eight miles to the west of it. He baptized people in the waters of Ullswater near the place where a nineteenth-century church now serves a rapidly growing holiday centre. Perhaps some of the people who came to him in repentance were 'the most unworthy, most evil and apostate Picts' to whom he likened those of his own countrymen who condoned the practice of traffic in slaves.

The Picts

These pagan Picts, first mentioned by the Roman orator Eumenius in 296, were popularly believed to have been given that name from the Greek *pikros*, referring to the way that they pricked or tattooed their bodies. They were the earliest Celtic Britons, and by 388 were organized and valiant enough to take their raiding parties as far south as London, although they were driven back across the wall in the following year. Despite that incursion they remain a mysterious people, and the greatest mystery about them is their disappearance from history after the ninth century. Although they used an Ogham script, they left no written records behind them apart from a list of their kings (proving a matrilineal succession) and a few names on grave slabs.

Pelagianism

As well as struggling with the pagan Picts, the Celtic Church of Patrick's time also had to contend with doctrinal differences. At the end of the fourth century, the teaching of the British monk Pelagius was stirring up bitter controversies in Rome. By 380, when his teaching was at the height of its power, many of Jerome's own disciples were among its followers and approved the doctrine which denied original sin and claimed that man was free to choose God and a virtuous life without being entirely dependent on Divine Grace. It was a doctrine that Rome felt compelled to crush, and in 429 Germanus and Lupis were sent to Britain to put an end to the heresy. They never succeeded and a strain of Pelagianism has always remained in the British character, although two hundred years later at the Synod of Whitby the Roman Church finally imposed its form of Church administration on the Celts.

This book is not about doctrine. It is concerned with the journeys which were made by the adherents of the Celtic Church over a period of three hundred years, from the time of Ninian in the fourth century to Cuthbert in the seventh. Their footsteps will lead us through Galloway and the western borders, as we trace the travels of Ninian and Kentigern from Cumbria to Strathclyde; up the length of Argyll and then across the Great Glen from Iona to Inverness in the wake of Columba and his companions; and finally through the eastern borders, from the Firth of Forth to Lindisfarne over the hills that Cuthbert knew.

The land we shall walk or drive over would not be recognizable to those early travellers. For one thing it is much safer. There is no need for us to worry about wolves, although that has only been the case for the last couple of hundred years. The last wolf in Scotland was shot in 1743. It was because of their presence that the Scots adopted the practice of burying their dead on islands, where the corpses would be safe from the prowling beasts. Although we shall come across many islands, quite apart from those used for burials, where holy men spent long periods in solitary retreat, there are few instances of any hermit living alone on the hills.

It was partly to clear out the wild beasts that many of the trees of the Caledonian Forest were felled. When the saints of the Columban Church travelled through Scotland they had to make their way through heavily wooded country where we now go across bare, eroded mountainsides. The forest meant that the climate of the Highlands was at least half as wet again as it is today. Burns which we can cross with ease would have been impassable rivers then. It is still possible to appreciate what they were like when a summer storm turns a trickle of water into a raging flood in a matter of minutes.

Unpredictable weather and geography make walking in Scotland, even south of the Great Glen, a serious adventure. It is important to be prepared for sudden mists or cold even on the hottest day. You should never set out without warm clothes, some food, a first-aid kit and the possibility of cover (a thick dustbin bag will do) in case you should be forced to spend a night on the mountain. Above all, make sure that somebody knows where you are bound for and roughly what direction you will take.

The appropriate sheet of the Ordnance Survey map is vital, and so is a compass. On open country you should constantly check your position. Most people take slightly longer steps with the right foot than they do with the left (that is why you walk in circles when you get lost) and it is all too easy to be heading northeast when you think you are walking due north. It is particularly important to check your direction carefully in Scotland, for you will find few tracks or footpaths marked on the map and none that relate to public rights of way. Within reason you may go where you will, but you can be sued for damage, and many places are so tightly wired round that it is impossible to get over a fence without damaging it.

At least the Celtic *peregrinati* did not have to face that problem, and it is one that should not overshadow your walks too seriously if you have planned your route carefully. Above all, these walks are for delight. When the historian and Celtic scholar Nora K. Chadwick asked herself what purpose there could be in looking back at the saints of the Dark Ages, she included their 'spiritual happiness' among the attributes of their lives which could inspire our present age. I would do so too.

The 'white martyrdom of exile' could cause Columba to cry out for his lost Ireland:

> *Were all the tribute of Scotia mine*
> *From its midland to its borders,*
> *I would give all for one little cell*
> *In my beautiful Derry.*

So he sighed, but we know he was to become just as enchanted with treeless Iona as he was with the oak groves of home. I am sure that mountains, lochs and rivers also held him in their spell.

When the mist comes down at four o'clock in the afternoon, or when all the midges in Scotland declare their indifference to any insect-repellent cream, I too have regretted leaving home. Not for long though. These times are always set off by a land whose shapes and colours beckon me farther along the way.

✢

CHAPTER ONE

St Ninian and Galloway

Whithorn is a small inland town at the southern end of the rich farming land of the Wigtown peninsula. Here Ninian was born some time in the second half of the fourth century. At first sight there seems to be nothing unusual about the place. Its wide main street is like many another in southern Scotland; but if you go through the archway that leads off it, you will find yourself standing on the site of one of the oldest Christian settlements in Britain. In the field opposite the modern church and the ruins of the medieval priory there once stood a university city whose student population equalled the number of people now living in the town.

As a young man, Ninian travelled to Rome, where, according to Bede, 'he had been regularly trained . . . in the faith and the mysteries of the truth' (*Ecclesiastical History*, Book III, ch. iv). In 397, when he was about thirty-five years old, he came back to his birthplace, and made it his base until his death in 432. There he founded his *muintirr* or settlement, apparently cooperating with an existing church and bishop. His form of settlement was unlike anything that had been seen in Britain before, yet it was to become the model throughout the Dark Ages.

Ninian based his system on that developed by St Martin of Tours, whom he is supposed to have visited as he journeyed north from Rome. He settled his monks in an arrangement of cells which enabled them to live in solitary reflection while at the same time sharing in a corporate life. It was a scheme that was particularly adapted to the Celtic way of life, and which enabled Ninian to equate the office of Ab – the spiritual chief of a group of Druidic Celts – with that of a Christian bishop.

In honour of his own teacher, he dedicated the first stone church to be built in Britain to Martin; and he called it Candida Casa as a reminder of the white hut which St Hilary gave to St Martin at

Poitiers. The town's present name is derived from the Saxon *hwitern*, which also means 'white house'. The memory of St Martin has never been lost in this place, for he is depicted in the designs on a twelfth-century brass reliquary displayed in the beautifully tended little museum in the priory grounds.

Apart from that and much earlier museum pieces, all that is left of Whithorn's glorious past is a rough field which covers the excavations which proved the existence of the college – the sacred ruins of Ninian's church and those of the twelfth-century priory. Over it all a modern church building presides.

Glasserton

The spirit of Ninian is more easily felt in the sea cave in the cliffs that overhang the rocky beach of Glasserton to the west of the Machars promontory. The name of the district – it has also been known as Glaston – links it in many people's minds with the Glastonbury of Somerset, whose wattle church was claimed as the first Christian building in Britain, as Ninian's is said to be the first in stone.

In common with his teacher Martin, and in the tradition of the Desert Fathers, Ninian sought regular solitary retreats. It was to this cave that he came. It is a wild and lonely place even today, and even in summer, for all that it is so close to farms and villages. Long after the saint's death the place was used by men who wanted to withdraw from the world for a while. The crosses they cut into its walls take their chance with the weather; but those on the stones which were found about its entrance at the end of the last century are now preserved in the priory museum.

The simplest way to reach this cave from Whithorn is to take the main road (A746) out of the town, turn left at the T junction, and look for the farm track on the right which leads to Physgill House [83:427367]. Here it is possible to park. From there a footpath through the beech woods leads to a stream flanked by yellow flags and red campion, which give way to thrift as you approach the sea. The entrance to the cave, a fissure in the Silurian rocks, is a few yards to the north. It is surrounded by boulders and overhanging rocks. A landslip in 1983 meant that, perhaps for the first time in its history, it had to be closed to pilgrims. Even so it is still possible to feel something of the spirit that must have moved the solitary Ninian as he looked south from here to the Isle of Man, sacred to Michael and the sea god; and west to the Rhinns of Galloway and the early Christian settlement of Kirkmadrine.

We can imagine the practical Ninian using some of the solitary hours he spent in his cave to plan his own travels, but before we follow him on these I should like to look briefly at two early accounts of his life, and at some other places besides Whithorn which he must have known in his native Galloway.

The first life is contained in an anonymous eighth-century Latin poem, *Miracula Nynie Episcopi*. This was included in an anthology compiled by the monk Alcuin (735–804) and mentioned by him in a letter to the monks of Candida Casa. If the fourteen chapters of the poem were actually written at Whithorn, then they form the earliest piece of Scottish literature that we have.

The poem starts off with an account of the founding of Ninian's settlement at Whithorn, and its indebtedness to the teaching of Martin. '*Martini haec meritus edis veneranda coruscat*' (From the goodness of Martin this shrine takes its holiness and splendour). One of the aspects of this holiness was the power of healing, and the poet tells us that many who had diseases of long standing hurried to Whithorn and there grew 'strong in all their limbs by the power of the saint'. The devotion that Ninian aroused in the people angered the secular ruler and so, like many a Celtic Christian before and after him, he was forced into exile. The brutal King Tuduael, who ordered his expulsion, was struck blind for that wicked deed, and so had himself to resort to the healing powers of the holy man.

In common with all early hagiographers, this anonymous poet gives much space to recounting the miracles of his subject. He claims that as well as having the gift of healing, Ninian could work such marvels as causing a day-old child to name its father (thus freeing a priest from a charge in a paternity case), and bringing a would-be cattle rustler back to life after he had been gored to death by a bull which was under the saint's protection.

Then the poem tells how Ninian went to Rome, climbing the Alps 'where milk-white fleeces glide in the silent sky, and the mountain peaks are buried in drifts of snow. Then he proceeded on sacred foot . . .' A later life of the saint compiled by Ailred, a Hexham priest who visited Galloway in 1164 according to the account of Reginald of Durham, and who eventually became abbot of Rievaulx, makes no

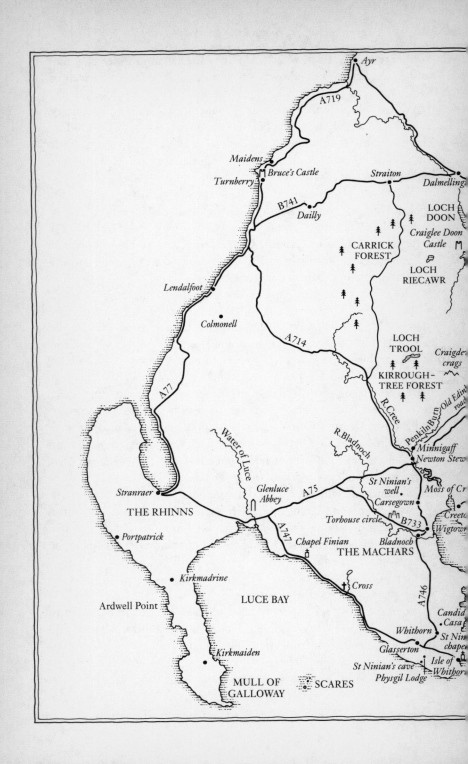

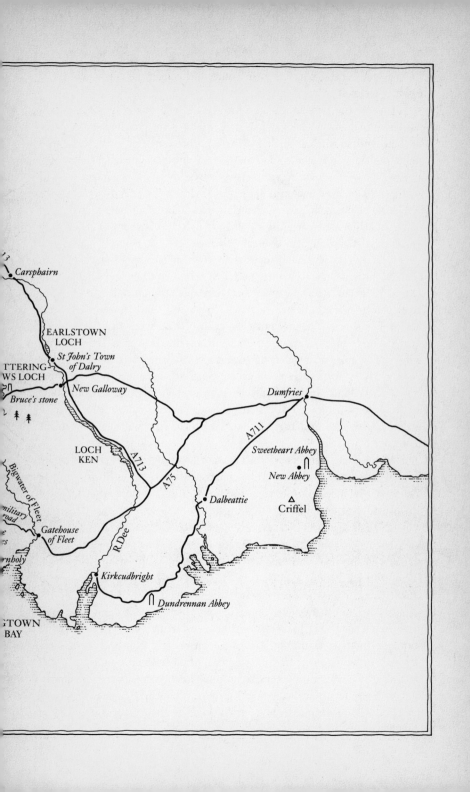

mention of Ninian's journey to Rome, but it does give an account of his visit to St Martin.

It is to Ailred's life that we owe much of our knowledge of Ninian's way of journeying. He was given to reading from holy works as he walked, and so long as he kept his thoughts pure, says his hagiographer, his open book would remain miraculously dry in the heaviest shower. When he journeyed across water he went in a coracle, and Ailred tells us how it would have been made from a frame of twigs in the form of a cup 'of such a size that it can contain three men sitting close together. By stretching an ox-hide over it, they render it not only buoyant, but actually impenetrable by water.'

The sea voyages called forth their own miracles. A young scholar of Whithorn was swept out to sea in a half-made coracle when he ran away in an attempt to escape Ninian's condemnation for some youthful misdemeanour. A storm blew up, but fortunately the lad had compounded his fault by taking the saint's holy staff with him on his flight. This proved to have the power of controlling wind and water; moreover, he found that it could be used as a mast, helm and anchor as the need arose. So that unseaworthy vessel was brought to land. Immediately the grateful youth planted the staff in the ground in token of his miraculous rescue, whereupon it grew roots, blossomed and turned into a healing tree with a fountain at its foot.

It is to Ailred, who claims that Ninian was born on the shores of the Solway Firth (which tradition has narrowed down to Whithorn), that we owe the information that the saint was the son of a king of Cumbria; later legend has it that his mother was a Spanish princess.

Although the saint is so closely associated with the Machars of the Wigtown peninsula, there is evidence of early Christian settlements to the west, on the southernmost section of the long spit of land which forms the Rhinns of Galloway. Christianity was established here at least half a century before Ninian's birth.

This is the closest part of mainland Britain to Ireland, and it is reasonable to allow the tradition that it was from somewhere near the modern Portpatrick that St Patrick journeyed to Ireland, although it is difficult to believe the most far-fetched of all Irish stories, which tells that he swam over the water carrying his head between his teeth after he had been decapitated by angry tribesmen. Whether or not Patrick received his training for the priesthood at Whithorn, and it is logical to imagine that he did, his final return to Ireland took place about three years after Ninian's death.

Kirkmadrine

Both Patrick and Ninian must surely have known the site of Kirkmadrine [82:086484]; for it was to become a holy place in the fifth century, as the stone crosses which have been found there prove. The seldom-used church, nine miles south of Stranraer, is now mainly a graveyard. It is set on a slight rocky outcrop, the path to it running between an avenue of trees which screen the cornfields on either side. I was there at harvest time, and the 'solitary reaper' did not think it necessary to wear earplugs to cut out the sounds from his transistor, but even that row could not completely obliterate the pleasant isolation of the place, although this is flat, rich farmland, unexciting except for the proximity of the sea, and that is invisible even from the slight elevation of the church.

In the porch, carefully preserved behind a shield of Perspex, are the ancient stones found on the site. Here is a rough square pillar marked with the Chi–Rho symbol, and commemorating in Latin 'the holy and chief priests' Ides, Viventius and Mavorius. It stands among seven other stones, the most recent of which dates from the twelfth century. The Latin inscriptions are fitting. Scholars like Nora Chadwick claim that it was the Romans who taught the Celts to cut stone, and these Christian crosses stem from that tradition.

Going south from here, the main road follows the eastern coastline of this narrow strip of land; but a more interesting route takes you by lanes and field paths to the coast, past the rocks of Ardwell Point and the Broch of Doon Castle [82:068447]. The ultimate goal is the village of Kirkmaiden, called for the ninth-century St Medan, an Irish princess who threw her eyes into Luce Bay rather than marry. The legend is that they became the rocks of the Scares, twelve miles out to sea, and that the caves on the shore of the Whithorn peninsula [82:364401] are also associated with her story. The ruins of one further church [82:138325] stand between here and the land's end of the Mull of Galloway. They are to be found beside a little stream in mechanically cultivated farmland.

Ninian and his monks stand midway in time between such modern agriculture with the heavy and noisy machinery that is familiar to us and the Neolithic and Bronze Age settlements that mark the Galloway coastline. The most impressive of those monuments lies to the east, between Creetown and Gatehouse of Fleet. The two burial chambers of Cairnholy [83:518542] are built on a similar plan to those found on the other side of the Irish Channel. They were in use from 3000 to 1800 BC. From the mound of the first chamber it is possible to look across Wigtown Bay towards Whithorn. The second cairn is a few yards to the north by some farm buildings. A small red stoat played by the farm fence as I climbed the mound and wondered about the people who were buried there and the landscape and creatures which made up their lives. In the hills to the north are the stone circles which mark their ritual meeting places. A farm road runs east from Kirkdale Burn and then heads north to the farm of Cloughreid; from there it goes across the hills to the old military road which once joined the Gatehouse of Fleet to Creetown. The most accessible of the stone circles is to the south of that road, and to the west of the Englishman's Burn at 83:508583.

Surely St Ninian and his monks paused at such early sacred sites as they set off north on their travels through Galloway to the lands beyond the Antonine Wall. Their long journey from Whithorn started with a crossing of the river Cree at a place which is now marked by the market town of Newton Stewart and the village of Minnigaff. From there a ridgeway runs to the north and east.

Two Irishmen, of the fifth century, whose names have come down to us, started along this way. One was Endam, who turned to the west, crossing the Galloway highlands to start a Christian community on the Isle of Arran. The other was Finnian or Finbar, a student at Candida Casa, who later founded his own community at Moville in Ireland where Columba came as a young man. It was Finnian who is thought to be responsible for the most northern of the St Ninian churches, whose site still carries that saint's name in Wick Bay in Caithness.

The extent of the work of these men, and of other monks from Candida Casa, can be measured in terms of the Ninian dedications all over Scotland, from Shetland to Stirling, and from Bute in the west to Aberdeenshire in the east. In Forfarshire there is a St Ninian Isle by Arbroath, and a well dedicated to the saint at nearby Arbirlot. There was a monastery at that place until the thirteenth century, and the early date at which the Christian settlement was made here is proved by a remarkable Pictish stone, unearthed in the nineteenth century. It stands in the garden of the Manse, and is marked with two small equal-armed crosses which the Reverend Douglas Simpson emphatically claimed show a clear influence of the Whithorn stones.

Perth's cathedral carries Ninian's dedication, and the tall, round, eleventh-century Irish-Celtic tower at the top of the school wynd by the church at Abernethy may indirectly owe its existence to the saint's teaching. For Abernethy was the capital of the kingdom of the Southern Picts, and according to the *Pictish Chronicle* the church there was dedicated to Bridget of Kildare in 462. In that year the king of the Picts handed the royal city over to Bridget's successor, the abbess of Darlingdach. This took place about thirty years after Ninian's death and a whole century before the Northern Picts accepted Christianity.

Glen Urquhart

Today one of the most beautifully sited of the Ninian churches is in Glen Urquhart on the west side of the Great Glen. Although the church by Loch Meiklie [26:434305] was only built in the mid-nineteenth century, its altar incorporates a St Ninian Cross on a stone slab. That stone was found at Kil St Ninian, a settlement which is still remembered in the name of St Ninian's Farm [26:528304] overlooking Loch Ness, and in that of Temple Pier [26:520300] which juts out into the water beneath it. This hillside is thought to have been the home of the first Christians in Glen Urquhart, and their sanctity was such that for centuries the well which they used was believed to have healing powers.

The travellers from Whithorn who took Ninian's teaching to the north started out along the route now followed by the Old Edinburgh Road, a pleasant green track leading out of the Machars to the wild highlands of Galloway, an area now covered by the Galloway Forest Park. It starts from Minnigaff, whose old ruined church with its medieval monuments and the McClurg stone, relating the story of the three half-brothers of Glen of Trool who set out to join the forces of the exiled Bruce, stands between the river Cree and the Penhiln Burn.

To the east a lane climbs up into the hills, the old road leaving the metalled lane to the north of a belt of trees. It then runs over the hills, keeping more or less parallel to the A712 as it makes its way to New Galloway. For a mile or so the Old Edinburgh Road goes along a treeless pastured ridge, and then enters the conifer forest of Kirroughtree. The old road runs above the knoll which carries the monument to Alexander Murray [77:489719], a self-taught shepherd boy, born on 22 October 1775, who became a professor of Oriental languages at Edinburgh. The ruins of the cottage of Dunkitterick in which he was born are in the plain, sheltered by the hills to the south. To reach it you have to climb down from the old way, possibly following the course of the Grey Mare's Tail waterfall (one of three in Galloway to be so called) and pass the fence of the wild goat reserve on Craigdew Crags. Although there is nothing very wild about these black and white shaggy beasts who queue up with their kids for the tourists' titbits during the summer months, they are attractive woolly creatures. The red deer in the reserve to the north of the one inhabited by the goats have not become so domesticated.

If you rejoin the old way to Edinburgh, you will find that it keeps to the ridgeway, going north round the little Black Loch and well to the south of Lilla's Loch. It runs beside the burn which joins a tributary of the Rulran Burn running into Clatteringshaws Loch. This idyllic bit of hillside, where little tan butterflies sport, is coloured with yellow broom and tormentil, the deep blue of the heath milkwort, and the reds and purples of stork's bill, heathers and lousewort.

Clatteringshaws Loch is largely an artificial reservoir, as you can tell from the great dam by the main road. When the waters were very low in 1974, a Celtic round house was discovered about half a mile to the northwest of the site of the Forestry Deer Museum [77:552764]. The round house dates from the time of the Roman occupation, but it may well have stood in an established settlement which Ninian would have known. A lane goes east round the edge of the loch to join the main road which passes the wooded promontory on which the museum stands. A little farther on in a clearing in the trees [77:558770] a large stone commemorates Robert Bruce's victory over the English army in 1307, in the battle of Raploch Moss. It is said that Robert Bruce lent against this stone while his followers gathered up the spoils.

From the southeastern tip of the loch, you can take the ten-mile Forest Drive through the modern Bennan Forest to the shores of Loch Ken and the glen in which, one stormy day, Burns, who really belongs to Galloway, composed his well-known 'Scots wha hae wi' Wallace bled'. That was when the place was truly a wild glen, and no main road ran along the west bank of the loch, past Kenmure Castle to New Galloway. The Old Edinburgh Road follows the course of the A712 fairly closely to the crossing of the Waters of Ken, then heads to the northeast. The way to the north and west goes by St John's Town of Dalry – an ancient royal place, for Dalry or Dalrigh signifies 'the king's meadow'.

A little farther north past Earlstoun Loch, and a mile past the bridge over the Polharrow Burn, an old packhorse road goes northwest along the way that was used by Ninian's missionaries journeying to Arran. Now the path from the road to the ridgeway is overgrown with bracken but it is worth persevering to reach the top of the hill, and the track which took prehistoric traders over Stroangassel Hill. Its later use as a pilgrim route is marked by two tenth-century crosses which stand by the site of a vanished wayfaring shrine to the south of Bardennoch Hill [77:572908]. It rejoins the main road at Carsphairn.

The real adventure across the rocks and peat bogs of the wild Galloway highlands starts a little to the north of that village at the lush vale of the Green Well of Scotland. From there a track to the disused mines runs between a stone circle to the north, and a hilltop cairn to the south. When the track fades, there is a difficult walk through new forestry planting to the banks and braes of Burn's Loch Doon. One of the caves overlooking this loch is among the many in which Bruce is supposed to have watched the spider whose dogged persistence gave him heart to continue his struggle against the English.

To the south of Loch Doon is a stretch of trackless country where 'lanes' are rushing burns. To get to the western shore of the loch you must cross one of them, and the waters of Gala Lane can be turbulent. Once across, you will find a path going north by the lochside to the ruins of Bruce's castle. These battered, circular walls, entered through an arched gateway, originally stood on an islet in the loch. When the hydroelectric power scheme caused the waters to be raised, the ruins were moved, stone by stone, and set up on the shore. In the drought of 1984, the waters of the loch fell so low that the island with the foundations of the original castle could once again be seen.

From the head of Loch Doon, a road goes north to the wild Ness Glen and the town of Dalmellington. From there the B741 runs to Straiton and the west. Another route starts off with the eight-mile walk through Carrick Forest to Craiglure, going along the forest road above Whitespout Lane and the head of Loch Reicawr to

Ballochbeatties and on to Stinchar Bridge, and the road which links Straiton and Newton Stewart. To the south are the lonely crags and desolate lochs of the Awful Hand range, culminating in the heights of Merrick. If time and weather hold, it is a place for memorable walks and climbs.

The Dark Age travellers, anxious to cross to the west by the simplest route, must have gone north to modern Dailly and over the hills to the Ayrshire coast. Here at the seaside village of Maidens are traces of Turnberry castle where Bruce was born and to which he returned when his Hebridean exile was over. From here you look across to Kildonan on the Isle of Arran, where the marytred saint Donan, who lived some two hundred years after Ninian, founded one of his settlements.

From Turnberry, the roads that Agricola built around AD 82 head south. At Colmonell north of Glen Tig, inland from Lendalfoot, there is a church that is linked both to Ninian himself and to another, later, saint, Colman of Eta, a nephew of St Columba. A thousand years later this village knew other men who felt so strongly about their faith that they were even prepared to die for it, a decision that Ninian's followers never needed to make. Matthew McIlwraith, one of the many Covenanting martyrs of Galloway and Ayrshire to be shot at Claverhouse's command in the killing time of the 1680s, lies in the graveyard.

Whithorn

Centuries before those fearful persecutions of Christians by Christians took place, the people of Galloway and pilgrims from far beyond that region were coming on pilgrimages to Whithorn, seeking the healing power that was to be experienced at Ninian's tomb. Some of the early cures that took place there are recorded by the anonymous eighth-century poet, who claimed to be speaking 'verses of truth revealing the miracles of the saint'.

He tells how the Whithorn monk Pethgils was brought to Candida Casa by his parents as a wretched, paralysed boy, expected to die there. Instead, he had a vision of the saint which immediately restored life to his limbs. Another story tells how a leper was cleansed as he prayed by the tomb of 'furrowed marble' in which the saint's body lay, itself a victim of that fateful, wasting disease. A woman was cured of blindness here, and finally the poet shows in triumphant lines how the priest Plecgils was granted a vision of Christ as he 'stood at the altar, a suppliant in prayer, where the bishop Nyniau, rejoicing in the Lord rests in the body in the tomb, while his spirit rejoices in splendour'.

A medieval life of the saint which has been ascribed to the Scottish poet Barbour, author of *The Bruce*, extolls Ninian in these lines:

> *For as a lantern he was lycht*
> *That in mirknes giffs men sycht.*

It was a light that was to draw thousands of people to Galloway. In 1427 James I gave protection to all the pilgrims who came there from England and Ireland, provided that they journeyed home by the same route as they came to Galloway. To ensure their safe conduct they had to wear the official pilgrim badge in their hats and restrict their visit to fifteen days.

The shrine drew its royal pilgrims. Before he became king, Edward II, in command of one of his father's armies, came to seek strength of the saint, whose image was removed by the angry Scots to New Abbey, only to be miraculously transported back to Whithorn before the prince arrived. Robert Bruce, no doubt mindful of the story of the earlier leper's cure, came to Ninian's tomb three months before his own death from that disease. David II, Edward's son, was more fortunate than his father, for he was granted relief when he prayed to the saint to remove an intractable arrowhead which had lodged in his body during his defeat at the battle of Neville's Cross. The Jameses III, IV and V of Scotland were all regular pilgrims to Whithorn. James IV went there almost every year, journeying with a great retinue and accompanied by minstrels. His last visit was in December 1512, nine months before he was to die on Flodden Field. Another tragic monarch to seek solace here was Mary, Queen of Scots, who came to Whithorn in August 1563.

The pilgrimages continue. The Holy Ghost Fathers of Motherwell organize them for city boys, who walk over a hundred miles to Whithorn; and on the last Saturday of August, the bishop of Galloway holds his own pilgrimage, which was a truly massive affair until the closure of the railway made the journey too difficult for many people. Of today's pilgrims, it is the members of the Greek Orthodox Church who hold Ninian in greatest reverence. He is one of the chief saints in their hierarchy, and many of them believe that he actually travelled to the Far East.

Most pilgrims have always approached Whithorn from the land, journeying south through the peninsula, and assembling south of Wigtown where the road crosses the river Bladnoch [83:421542]. In 1441, Margaret, Countess of Douglas, was even forced to rebuild the bridge 'where pilgrims to St Ninian assemble', petitioning the Pope for an indulgence for her pains. Some pilgrims, especially those from Ireland and the Isle of Man, came to Whithorn by sea, sailing up the Solway Firth to the harbour sheltered by the Isle of Whithorn, which is now joined to the mainland by a causeway. There is evidence that Ninian made a settlement on the more westerly of the two little hills which form the island, and where the earthworks of a hill fort may be traced. On the slopes of the other hill are the roofless remains of a late-thirteenth-century chapel. It stands in a walled enclosure, fenced off from the grazing cattle. This chapel replaced an earlier one whose existence is confirmed by the traces of a narrow chancel and of a chancel arch dating from the twelfth century or earlier. That building, in which the pilgrims gathered to recover from the sea crossing before walking the few miles north to Whithorn, was probably damaged during Edward I's attacks on Scotland.

Glenluce Abbey

In its function as a pilgrim's rest, that little chapel was in some ways comparable to the great Glenluce Abbey to the northwest [82:184587]. Glenluce's last abbot was Thomas Hay, whose son built the stark Castle of Park in 1590. Today these abbey ruins are among the most gentle in Scotland. In high summer they are covered in stonecrop and alpine fairy foxglove, while all around the roadsides are thronged with deep colonies of the tall purple spears of our native breed.

James IV made Glenluce a stopping place on at least two of his visits to Whithorn; and before his time, Bruce was here, sick and mourning the death of his beloved wife Elizabeth, who had died while on a pilgrimage of her own to the northern sanctuary of the tenth-century St Duthac at Tain. These kings were only two of the thousands of people who sheltered in this Cistercian abbey since it was founded by Rolland, Lord of Galloway, in 1192.

St Finnian

Another site at which pilgrims assembled was the chapel of St Finnian on the western coast of the Whithorn peninsula [82:278489]. The substantial ruins of that chapel are separated from the rocky coast by the road and are easy to reach. Like all early Celtic churches, it was originally a rectangular building, measuring some 14 by 18 feet.

From here the route across the hills to Whithorn is marked by the cross in the woods to the south of the White Loch of Myrton [83:355429]. This highway was frequented long before the pilgrims came, as can be seen from the cairns, earthworks and tall standing stones that cluster round the hillside to the north of Chapel Finnian, and from the cup-and-ring-marked rocks to the north of the loch and the stone circle [83:363420] to the south of it.

Ardwall Island [83:573495] west of Kirkcudbright was another pilgrims' resting place. Here a tenth-century stone slab marked with an incised cross was found in the 1920s. The island also bears evidence of earthworks that could be the remains of a small chapel belonging to a monastic settlement connected with Whithorn, and later transferred to the domain of Iona. Medieval pilgrims from England and the east may have stopped there after following the coast road south from Dumfries towards their earlier resting place at Sweetheart Abbey, whose red sandstone ruins stand among the houses of the village of New Abbey. The abbey was founded in the thirteenth century by Devorgilla, daughter of Galloway's last Celtic lord. She married a Norman, John de Baliol, Bruce's rival and king of Scotland for four years from 1292. Devorgilla so loved her husband that when he died she brought his heart from Barnard Castle in Teesdale and carried it with her in a silver casket so that it should be buried with her on the shores of the Solway.

A hundred years before the founding of Devorgilla's abbey, the pilgrims went southwest from Dumfries by the road through the plain, which is flanked to the southeast by a little group of hills. The highest of these is Criffell, which rises to 1866 feet. It is crowned with two large cairns, one of which is known as the Douglas Cairn, claiming its name from the story that the Black Douglas died when his horse stumbled at this place. In fact he was killed when taking Bruce's heart to the Holy Land and his link with the hill is more likely to have come from his choice of this site for setting up one of the balefires which gave warning of English attacks from across the water.

Now the A711 runs to Dalbeattie and on from there to the ruins of Dundrennan Abbey, founded in 1142 by Devorgilla's ancestor Fergus, Lord of Galloway. For many years this was one of the most powerful abbeys in southern Scotland, even possessing its own fleet of ships. So it is reasonable to see it as a resting place for many of the pilgrims to Whithorn. Some of them may have sailed to the site of Ninian's tomb from St Cuthbert's town of Kirkcudbright, but most must have crossed the Cree estuary by Creetown and made their way south from there. If you follow in their steps you will have your first encounter with Ninian at one of several wells dedicated to him in this region. This one is by the A714 at the north of the Moss of Cree. From the well the road goes through rich farmland, low-lying to the east, slightly hilly to the west, where there is plenty of evidence that the people of the Bronze Age also found this a good place to settle.

Another St Ninian Well can be reached from the farm of Carsegowan [83:420588] by following the farm road that goes directly south. A little to the north of this well, a track goes west past two cairns on Auchleand Moor and on to the farm tracks which run south to Torhousemuir and the B733. A few hundred yards to the west along that road you will find the Bronze Age circle of Torhouse, its centre adorned with three separate standing stones. The whole monument is in a sort of cage by the roadside.

The pilgrims would have been unlikely to make that detour. Their route went directly south from the well (and a footpath still marks the way) to the crossroads to the north of the bridge of Bladnoch. From there they might have been briefly tempted off the route by going east to Wigtown. It stands near the sea, a mile or so off the main road, and you enter it through a large central square. The church is to the north of the town, and in its churchyard is a long ivy-covered ruin. If you look behind that you will find a memorial to one of the most tragic of the martyrs to perish for allegiance to the Covenant. Margaret Wilson was eighteen when she was forcibly drowned in 1685. Her story is briefly told in rhyming couplets on her grave: 'With the sea ty'd to a stake/ She suffered for Christ Jesus sake.' It was on Wigtown sands that she was forced to stand, waiting for the relentless tide to end her life.

Margaret's tragic and unnecessary death would have been incomprehensible to the monks of Whithorn, who knew the violence of the elements, who suffered attacks from wild beats on their journeys, and who sometimes may have had good reason to be afraid of the surrounding Picts, but who could imagine nothing like the killing times of the seventeenth century when men slaughtered each other for divergences in Christian beliefs. The gospel that Ninian preached was one of kindness; and his teaching was to influence all the other men whose journeys we are to follow. In the southeast, Serf (of Culross, on the northern shores of the Firth of Forth) accepted his teaching and passed its essence on to Kentigern, Glasgow's St Mungo.

✝

The Journeys of Kentigern

Kentigern's story begins in the rich farmlands of Lothian to the east of Edinburgh, for his maternal grandfather is said to have been the almost legendary King Loth, who gave his name to the region. His palace, historically recorded as Dunpedr, was the hill fort commonly known as Dun Pelder at the top of the Traprain Law [67:580747], a shapely outcrop of volcanic rock jutting out of the surrounding plain. Although Loth never seems to have been a Christian, Traprain Law has become intertwined with the story of the early Church, a tradition that stems perhaps from the belief that in the sixth century the virgin saint Modwena established her church here.

That bit of piety is probably as apocryphal as the legends surrounding Kentigern's conception and birth. To appreciate the story to its full you first need to climb this strange uneasy piece of rock. The path leading up to the earthworks which surrounded the palace enclosure starts from a stile to the west of the quarry which has eaten away the northeastern slope of the hill, and which would indeed have destroyed the whole eminence if a stop had not been put to the quarrying in 1980.

Across the stile a footpath leads through the high grasses, gently circling the northern contours of the hill, then turning east for a steeper climb to the western entrance to the fort. Here the hillside is disturbed by a mass of stones that have fallen from the old ramparts, which excavations in the early years of this century proved to have taken the form of 12-foot-high turf walls faced with stone. They encircled an area of some forty acres, protected by inner ramparts.

The heights of Traprain Law, 710 feet above sea level, seem peaceful enough on a summer day. Sheep graze among the yellow bedstraw and the cloudy brown-purple Yorkshire fog, yet there is a slightly uneasy feeling to the place; which may account for the stories that have grown up around it. The profusion of nettles tells of long

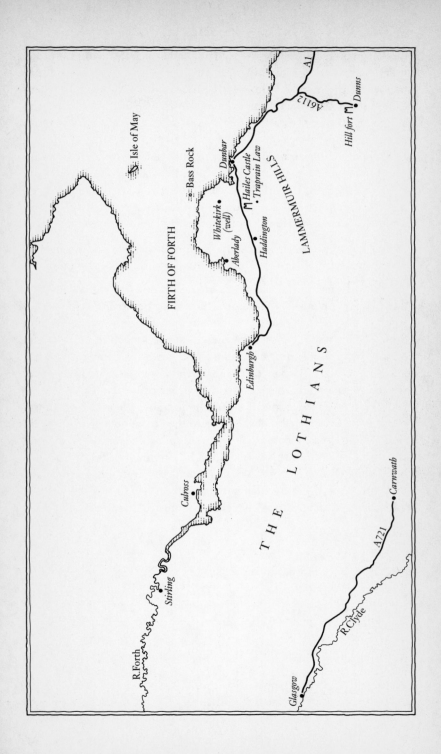

Isle of May

Bass Rock

FIRTH OF FORTH

Dunbar

A1

A6112

Hill fort ⌂ • Duns

LAMMERMUIR HILLS

Hailes Castle ⌂
Trapain Law •

Whitekirk
(well)
Aberlady •

Haddington •

THE LOTHIANS

Edinburgh •

Culross •

Carnwath •

A721

R.Clyde

R.Forth

Stirling •

Glasgow •

human habitation, and it is easy to imagine people living here, for there is a water supply within the enclosure, albeit reduced in summer to a swampy rectangle. Whoever lived here in the distant past did so in some splendour and with some contact with the world at large, for the animal figures on the pottery that was discovered here resemble those found in Egypt.

So Dun Pelder on Traprain Law must have been a place of wonder to the men and women who spent hard lives tilling the fields of the plain or fishing in the firth; and when the great palace was abandoned in the fifth century, it is small wonder that stories should have grown up around it. The best-known of these concerns Kentigern's conception.

Thanew

A very early account of the saint's life tells how Loth had a daughter, Thanew or Thaneukes (a name which later became transmuted to Enoch, and as such she is remembered in Glasgow in St Enoch's Square). She was a girl of such piety that she longed to emulate the Virgin Mary in all things, including the power to conceive without knowing a man. A man of noble birth, Ewen, son of Ewegende, wished to marry her, but against the wishes of her father she steadfastly refused such a convenient and honourable alliance. Her refusal so added to Ewen's desire that he determined to come to her by a trick. By dressing up as a woman he was able to trap her into being alone with him, and when this was achieved he immediately impregnated her. To the chronicler, such a rape maintained her innocence, while at the same time bringing such suffering upon her as was due for the 'presumption of her vanity' in trying to compare herself to the Mother of Christ.

Her sufferings were sharp enough, for it was the custom of that time that any noble woman who committed fornication was to be stoned. As none of her executioners could bring himself to cast the first stone at her body, she was put in a wagon and brought to the sheer southern scarp of Traprain Law. The wagon was pushed backwards over the cliff. Then the first of the miraculous happenings in Kentigern's life took place, for the wagon with his mother inside it righted itself in its fall and brought her safely to the ground, the pole becoming fixed in the earth. When that was drawn out, a fountain sprang from the soil.

The miracle did nothing to soften the heart of Loth, who was more determined than ever to get rid of his shameful daughter. So he ordered that she should be put in a coracle and cast adrift in the waters of the Firth of Forth. To that end she was taken three miles north across the plain to the sea at Aberlady.

That place is now a genteel seaside town (albeit threatened by the nuclear waste that is dumped nearby), standing by a wide estuary of mud flats; but it was once a great harbour, and as late as the nineteenth century there were fears that Napoleon would use it as a landing place. Kentigern's earliest biographer knew the estuary as the Mouth of Stench – Aberlessic – because of the quantities of fish that were left to rot there, for the catches in these waters were so vast that men were unable to handle them. It was at that spot that Thanew was consigned to the waters.

If we leave the wretched girl tossing in the coracle as it was swept east towards the Isle of May, which is now a notable gathering place for seals, we can look a little longer at the troubled borderland of Lothian, which has the first claim on Glasgow's Mungo. He is not the only saint of this land, for in the eighth century it was sought out by Baldred, a hermit from Northumbria, who settled at Tyninghame and later on the Bass Rock [67:603873], which is of the same volcanic formation as Traprain Law. His well in the parish of Whitekirk attracted thousands of pilgrims who claimed to be cured of barrenness there. In an excess of Protestant zeal it was closed and sealed up in 1815.

A little to the south, the very ordinary, rather depressing seaside town of Dunbar has a long role in Lothian's history. In the mid-seventh century there was an Anglian palace here; and in the Middle Ages Dunbar's castle, now a few jagged ruins of red sandstone, jutted out to sea, linked by easily defended bridges to the rock stacks off the shore. From here it was possible to protect or attack the route south across the Lammermuirs, and in the changes of fortune that struck this turbulent borderland both functions were needed.

We find other military installations along Lothian's highways. On the south bank of the River Tyne, at the northern foot of Traprain Law are the ruins of Hailes Castle, sited to defend the land and water routes running east to west. Until 1567 this castle was held by the Hepburn family, but at that date it passed into the hands of James, fourth Earl of Boswell. And so it came about that the unfortunate

Mary, Queen of Scots, stayed here on her way to imprisonment in Dunbar Castle after Boswell had abducted her in Edinburgh on 24 March of that year.

In the south, across the Lammermuirs, above the town of Duns where the Franciscan John Duns Scotus was born in 1266, there is another hill fort guarding the route to the south [67:785547]. From its heights, covered in delicate pink parslane, you can look out over the Cheviots, as Loth's people must have done. But now we are dragged out of the Dark Ages to face the tragic conflicts of the Covenanters, whose fate in 1639, the year after the Scottish National Covenant was formed, is recorded on a stone here. In taking a stand against episcopacy, they were in some measure returning to the arrangements of the Celtic Church, which regarded bishops of far less account than the abbots and the voices of the communities they presided over.

Another martyr of those times was Montrose's chaplain, George Wishart, who, escorted and succoured by John Knox, met his death a little to the north, in what is now the elegant Georgian town of Haddington. This was the birthplace of two stalwart but contrasting Victorians, Jane Welsh Carlyle and Samuel Smiles.

The latter would have been pleased with the endurance of his strange countrywoman Thanew, although it was not by self-help alone that she got through her ordeal. Her coracle reached the Isle of May in safety, escorted thither by all the fish from Aberlady, who henceforth departed from that estuary, so that, in the words of the chronicler, 'the river mouth, so prolific in fish as mentioned above, because it received the child unjustly condemned, remaineth unproductive unto the present day'.

Kentigern

From the island, Thanew's course went for thirty miles west to the northern shore of the Firth of Forth, and in safety she landed at Culross. Here, although she was already in the throes of labour, she had the initiative and courage to light a little fire on the shore. Beside it Kentigern was born, and it was here that mother and child were found by some shepherds, who cared for them. And so the saint's birth has some of the traditional elements that surround the birth of a saviour. Like Moses he came from the water, like Mithras and Christ he was first seen by shepherds. In this case they ran with the news to

30

the holy Servanus, who had already had intimations of a wonderful birth, for at the time that the child was brought forth he had heard a *Gloria in excelsis* sung by a heavenly choir as he prayed in his oratory after the morning lauds. So his immediate response to the shepherds was 'Thanks be to God, for he shall be my dear one [Mungo]'. When he later baptized the baby he gave him his formal name of Kentigern, the Capital Lord.

The only reminder of Kentigern at Culross now is the remains of a St Mungo Chapel, erected by Robert Blackadder, the first bishop of Glasgow, in 1503. It stands a little outside the main town, by the waterside; but visitors do not seek it out. Instead they come in their thousands to walk round the little sixteenth-century town, which has been beautifully preserved by the Scottish National Trust. Its cobbled streets lead up to the abbey, built on the place where Servanus had his cell and where the infant Kentigern was brought up. The modern stained glass here shows both saints and tells the story of the finding of the baby.

Servanus or Serf, who taught and nurtured the young Kentigern, is sometimes confused with a later holy man of the same name who had a monastery on Loch Leven, where the Culdee Church did not yield to Rome until the twelfth century. The sixth-century Servanus of Culross, whose reputed remains were found in that village in 1530, is thought to have been a disciple of the fifth-century Saint Palladius. Many stories were told of Servanus' miraculous powers. It was said that after eating a piece of bacon he was able to restore the whole pig to life; and that a thief, who denied eating a sheep that he had stolen, was found out when the saint caused the sheep to bleat in his throat.

Jocelyn

This was the man who looked after the infant Kentigern. In the words of Jocelyn, a twelfth-century monk of Furness, who compiled the saint's life at the request of Herbert, bishop of Glasgow, he 'educated the child of God, like another Samuel committed unto him and assigned by God. But the child grew, and was comforted, and the grace of God was in him. But when the age of intelligence, and the acceptable time for learning arrived, he handed him over to be trained in letters, and spent much labour and care that he might profit in these things.'

Jocelyn is said to have wandered through the streets and lanes of Glasgow seeking records of that city's saint. He claimed to have based his biography on an ancient document in the cathedral church, which contained statements adverse to sound Roman doctrine, and so opposed to the Catholic faith. It must have been compiled by the Culdees, the followers of the Celtic Church who, for several centuries after the Synod of Whitby, refused to follow the practices of Rome. The word 'Culdee' is usually taken to mean 'the servants of God', but Jocelyn derived it from 'Cuiltich', 'the men of the recesses', disciples of Kentigern who devoted much of their lives to solitary retreats.

It is to Jocelyn that we owe the stories of the young Kentigern's miracles at the monastery of Culross, where he was found to have the power of restoring the dead to life, and used it for the benefit of the settlement's old cook and a tormented robin. Less dramatic, but more significant for his later life, was the time when a swathe of hazel twigs caught fire of their own accord when it was Kentigern's turn to light the lamps in the church, which he would not otherwise have been able to do, for his companions had put out all the fires from which he could have taken a flame. That the other boys had acted in such a way shows their jealousy of Kentigern's piety and of the special affection which he received from Servanus. Kentigern's response to that difficulty was to withdraw from Culross altogether; and as he decided to do so, it is said that the waters of the Forth parted. So he walked dry-shod where once he had tossed *in utero* in Loth's coracle.

Jocelyn called the place of his crossing Serf's Bridge, for Servanus is supposed to have followed his protégé, and to have been persuaded with difficulty that Kentigern was right to set out on his own mission. Probably, in fact, Kentigern, a young man just over twenty, feeling that it was time to set forth on his missionary journeys, left Culross by going inland and, crossing the Forth near Stirling, set out south and east on the road which was to bind him for ever to Glasgow. The legends tell us that on the very day that he parted from Servanus, Kentigern came to Carnwarth, and there met Fergus, an old man who had long prayed that he might see the saint before he died. His prayer having been granted, he happily left this life, and his body was put on a cart drawn by a team of young bulls who were otherwise unharnessed. He was to be buried wherever the animals stopped, and so the beasts drew him to the banks of a tributary of the Clyde, and would go no farther once they had reached an old cemetery blessed by Ninian.

This was the beginning of Glasgow (the name means 'a beloved green place'), and it was by Fergus's grave that Kentigern first hung up his handbell on the branch of a tree and called the people to a prayer. This story was told to explain the fact that, as a very young man, Kentigern was consecrated and elected as the first bishop of Strathclyde.

From here he probably conducted the missionary journeys to the northeast, traces of which are to be seen in the Kentigern dedications in Aberdeenshire. The pious believe that, in order to fit himself for these undertakings, he spent the whole season of Lent in solitary prayer. In any case he led an austere life. Jocelyn tells us that he lived sparsely on bread, milk, butter, cheese and pulses, and that he took frequent fasts. Whenever he ate at royal tables he intensified his austerities afterwards. He wore simple clothing, with a rough itchy garment next to his skin. At night he lay in a stone trough hollowed like a coffin. He had the power of silence, speaking seldom but always with effect, and his expression was generally cheerful. The staff he carried was of plain wood.

Yet, despite his saintly life, Kentigern could not face the persecutions of Morken, the pagan ruler of Strathclyde, and so he retreated south to Carlisle. From there he continued with his work, preaching to the people of Cumbria as he went until he came to North Wales, where the tradition is that, with the help of his young disciple Asaph, he founded the Christian settlement that now bears the latter's name.

The Battle of Arderydd

He was not to settle there indefinitely. After the battle of Arderydd in 573, when the Christians defeated the pagan forces at a place which has been equated with Arthuret on the banks of the River Esk, the new king, Rhydderch Hael, sent for Kentigern to return from Wales. We can join the saint on his return home as he went through Cumbria revisiting the churches he had established during his journey south. Near Keswick, it is good to imagine him speaking to the people from the old sacred site of Castlerigg, before he set out on the last stages of his journey to Strathclyde. In this circle of stones, reflecting the shape of the hills around them, there is a small rectangular enclosure which has baffled generations of archaeologists. I like to think that Kentigern spoke from there.

But that is all speculation. It is, however, very likely that he would

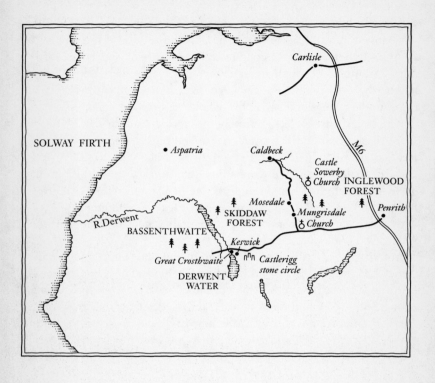

CARLISLE

SOLWAY FIRTH

Aspatria

Caldbeck

Castle
Sowerby
Church

INGLEWOOD
FOREST

M6

Mosedale

SKIDDAW
FOREST

Mungrisdale
Church

Penrith

R.Derwent

BASSENTHWAITE

Keswick

Great Crosthwaite

Castlerigg
stone circle

DERWENT
WATER

have gone straight to Great Crosthwaite, where twenty years previously he had planted a cross in the clearing of the valley between Bassenthwaite Lake and Derwent Water. The present church on that site on the outskirts of Keswick mostly dates from the sixteenth century heavily overlaid with nineteenth-century restoration, although a few traces of a twelfth-century building remain. Beside the Dark Age saint, two eminent Victorians are remembered here: the poet Robert Southey, whose grave in the churchyard was restored surprisingly enough by the Brazilian government in 1961; and Canon Rawnsley, vicar of this church for thirty-four years from 1883, but better remembered as the founder of the National Trust.

Tracing other Kentigern churches in Cumbria takes us northeast to Mungrisdale (St Mungo's Dale). The road runs north between Keswick and Penrith, the fells of Skiddaw Forest to the west and the plain of Inglewood to the east. In the village of Mungrisdale itself, a church which was most probably founded by Kentigern has stood overlooking that plain since 550. Here the saint's memory is kept alive in a banner which recalls his miracles, designed by Ella Kidd, who teaches theatre wardrobe design in Liverpool.

The next Kentigern church stands across the lowlands at Castle Sowerby. They say of this church, which almost stands in the yard of isolated Sowerby Hall, that any parson who can find it can have the living. I was fortunate in meeting a lady in Mungrisdale church who had been married at Castle Sowerby and could tell me how to reach that church, by taking the green lane and footbridge which crosses the stream flowing round the little hill on which both church and farm stand. It was in its waters that Kentigern is said to have baptized his converts.

The siting of this church suggests that, whether this was a Kentigern foundation or not, it stands on ground that was holy long before the thirteenth century, which is the date at which the list of rectors starts. In 1703, Bishop Nicolson recorded that there was a piece of stained glass relating to Kentigern in the north window, but it is no longer there.

You will need to return west to the fells, taking the road that goes through the village of Mosedale, where an early Quaker meeting house has been lovingly restored by the Wigton Friends. It serves as a coffee house and bookshop on summer weekdays. At this place you are about halfway from Mungrisdale to Kentigern's church at

Caldbeck, where the famous hunstman, John Peel, who died at Ruthwaite on 13 November 1854 at the age of seventy-eight, is buried. Again, there is a well near the present church, which dates in part from the twelfth century and was restored in 1932

From Caldbeck, it would seem from the number of Kentigern dedications along the northwest coast of Cumbria that the saint went west to Aspatria, and then worked his way round the southern shore of the Solway Firth to Carlisle. From there we can follow him along the northern shore to Annan, from where he must have made his way along one of the two Roman roads running through the Lowther Hills to the Clyde.

A hundred years after Kentigern's death, the Angles who then owned the territory as part of Northumbria erected a 17-foot-high cross on the shore at Ruthwell by Annan. It is inscribed with runes which spell out *The Dream of the Rood*, a poem glorifying Christ as a Saxon hero. Once the cross stood proudly by the wide sands of the firth, whose gold is rivalled in spring by the brilliance of the gorse. Now it is preserved in Ruthwell Church, reached by going inland from the B724 to the west of Annan. The keys to the building hang on a hook by the back door of the cottage at the junction between the road and the church lane.

Going farther inland, the B725 runs north towards Dalton and from there to the place where an oddly shaped hill rises above the river Annan. The best approach to this hill is from the lane opposite the back entrance to Hoddum Castle, whose grounds are now given over to a fairly well-hidden caravan site. In many ways, Hoddum should be to Kentigern what Whithorn is to Ninnian; indeed, it was a holy place in the early Middle Ages and the monastery that was set up there survived the worst of the Viking raids on Strathclyde and Galloway. Now the only reminder of its former importance is a ninth-century cross with an *agnus dei* crosshead, and even that is not on its original site, but displayed at the National Museum of Antiquity in Edinburgh.

The narrow footpath through the small wood opposite the castle entrance leads to a hill whose summit is reached by a short, steep climb across a field to a gaunt, square building which glowers across the surrounding country. It is aptly inscribed the Tower of Repentance, and it seems fitting that it should guard a gloomy burial ground. It is here that Kentigern is thought to have set up his first

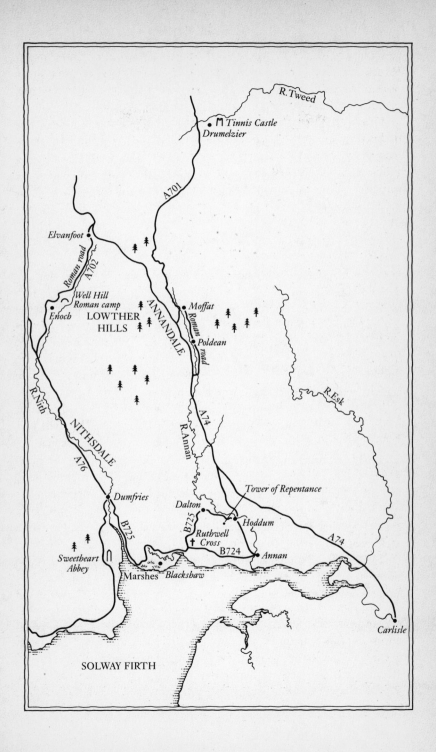

church, and even miraculously to have created the mound on which it stands. The chronology seems a little odd, as the miracle took place through his meeting with the king on his return from exile.

The story is that it was at this place that Kentigern first met the victorious Rhydderch. The crowds that came to see that great event were so large that most people had no hope of even catching a glimpse of their secular and spiritual leaders. As they craned and jostled in a desperate attempt to see what was going on, the ground on which the two men were standing raised itself above them and took on the shape of the present hill.

Merlin

Kentigern had one other less happy encounter at Hoddum, for the legend goes that he met a wild and infuriated Merlin here. It is very possible that the story grew out of an actual confrontation between the saint and one of the chief Druid priests from among the people whom Rhydderch had defeated at Arthuret, on the Blackshaw marshes. In that battle, Merlin is supposed to have won a gold torque, but to have lost his wits, so that he went through the surrounding countryside like a beast 'naked and outcast, fed only on the pasture of the herbage'.

Kentigern's most significant meeting with the Druid, however, took place well to the north of Hoddum, at Drumelzier by the River Tweed, to the west of Peebles. The road that runs through the village was guarded until the sixteenth century by Tinnis Castle, a fortification standing on the site of a hill fort to the east of the settlement, and perched on a rocky eminence which juts out above the watermeadows and below the hills of Tweedsmuir. The path to the hill fort and castle ruins goes through a cottage garden and then across a ladder set over a field wall and leading to the open moor.

Drumelzier is one of several places where Arthur's Merlin is supposed to be buried. In this case the story goes that Kentigern actually converted the crazed Druid here. Newly baptized in the waters of the Tweed, Merlin received the sacrament with joy and then, rather spitefully one might think, turned to the very aged saint and said, 'Father if today my life in the world should be completed . . . the most holy of bishops and the most noble of the nobility will follow me this year.' Shortly afterwards Merlin did indeed meet his death at the hands of his enemies, who stoned him and threw his body into the river. 'Wonder not,' says the writer of the *Scotichronicon*, 'that Merlin and St Kentigern died in one and the same year, for he was 181 when he died.' The great age is meant to refer to the saint, who indeed seems to have had a long and active life after Rhydderch recalled him from exile.

The Roman roads from the Solway to the north converge at Elvanfoot on the A74 to the southwest of Drumelzier. The western route from Dumfries reaches that place by routes that are covered by main roads through Nithsdale until the village of Enoch is reached. Here, in the place that remembers Kentigern's mother in its name, the ancient track runs to the northeast across the hills, past the Roman encampment on Well Hill. The eastern route to the north from Annan is covered by the A74 until it reaches the point where a lane crosses the railway to the south of the village of Poldean. From there you can follow it across the hills a little to the west of Moffat. Kentigern and his followers must have been familiar with both routes.

It was possibly along one of those roads that the saint returned to the north from his last journey, settling for the rest of his life on the banks of the Clyde. The stories of his final years relate to his life near the court of the king. The group of miracles performed at this time are all connected with the court. The first shows his human kindness in retrieving a ring which Rhydderch had given to his queen, Languoreth, and which she had given to her lover. Knowing what had happened, the king, who had somehow got hold of the ring, threw it into the Clyde, sentencing his wife to death if she could not produce it within three days. St Kentigern prayed, and in answer a salmon was caught with the ring in its stomach. After that it must have been almost as easy to turn sand into corn and to find mulberries at Easter for the court jester.

Like many other holy men, Kentigern had a deep respect and love for animals, and they were instinctively aware of his authority. As an example, the story is told of the wolf who did penance for killing a stag, by allowing himself to be harnessed to the saint's plough.

Kentigern lived to be extremely old, even if he did not reach the 181 years that some hagiographers credit him with. At any rate, he lived until he became so tired that he longed to leave this earthly life. The Lord, knowing his desire, directed him to prepare a warm bath and, in the comforting waters, at dawn in the week after Epiphany his spirit was separated from his body. He died comforted by a vision of the glory of the Lord, and 'conversing to the last with an attendant angel.'

Columba

Some time after his return from exile he seems to have met Columba. The stories tell how Columba came to Glasgow. However, Kentigern is supposed to have spent six months at Dunkeld in the abbey founded from Iona and they could have met there. The actual meeting probably took place at some point on the western end of the Antonine Wall.

It was a processional encounter. The saints approached each other, preceded by their youngest disciples. When they came together they exchanged their pastoral staffs. The one that Columba gave to Kentigern was inlaid with gold, and was preserved in the cathedral church at Ripon up to the fifteenth century.

The story of the encounter is told by Kentigern's biographer, the twelfth-century Jocelyn, but ignored by Adomnan, who wrote Columba's life only a century after the saint's death. That does not necessarily throw doubt on the authenticity of the episode, for Adomnan was more interested in accounts of miracles and discussions of doctrine than in recounting chronological events. It would seem strange, however, if these two beloved leaders, born within a year of each other, had never spoken together.

✦

CHAPTER THREE

Columba and the Way to Iona

The traditional birthday of Columba is 7 December 521. The day was a Thursday, and for centuries that day of the week has been considered an especially fortunate one in the Scottish Highlands, as an auspicious time to start any important enterprise. I am reminded too of the English 'Thursday's child has far to go' for, like his fellows, Columba was an intrepid traveller on land and sea, although it was not until he was over forty that he left his native Ireland.

He was born at Garton in Donegal into the clan of Cinel Conaill. Grandson of Fergus, who ruled over much of Donegal, and son of Fedlimidh, the chief of the clan, he was of royal descent in the line of the Niall of the Nine Hostages who ruled from 379–405. His mother Eithne understood that her pregnancy was momentous when she was given an intimation of her son's destiny before his birth. It came in a dream in which an angel gave her a cloak beautifully woven of all the colours in nature. This cloth spread out from all the mountains, loughs and forests of Ireland until it reached Scotland, and so covered all the land from County Mayo to Burghead on the Moray Firth. I wonder if she realized that she too was to journey to Scotland, as it appears she did, for she is supposed to be buried on the tiny holy island that is a part of the chain of the Garvellachs, the Isles of the Sea, which are reached from Easedale in Argyll.

As a boy, Columba studied under Finnian of Moville, and when he was in his early twenties he founded his own monastery at Derry. Always a man of immense energy, he found time in days that were largely given up to worship, administration and acts of human kindness to transcribe manuscripts. It was that last activity which was to be the immediate cause of his exile from Ireland, although there were, no doubt, other more serious political disputes that forced such a controversial statesman and churchman to leave the country.

Still, the story goes that, when he took 'the white martyrdom' of voluntary exile in 561, he did so as a penance for slaughtering the people of Clan Neill at the battle of Culdreimhne. That battle was Columba's immediate and furious response to the judgement of the high king, Diarmid, who had denied his right to make a copy of a psalter belonging to Finnian. Finnian maintained that the transcript was made without his permission and therefore belonged to him. Columba's case was that he had made the book for the general good and that in doing so he had done no harm to the original; he could find no reason why he should not make and keep a copy. It was this dispute that the two priests took to Diarmid, who immediately made the first pronouncement of copyright: 'To every cow its calf and to every book its copy.' It was then that Columba gathered his followers and tribesmen around him to do battle in his cause. As for the psalter he had made, it was discovered in a reliquary which was opened in 1813 and found to contain a copy of the Psalms, from Psalm 30, x, to Psalm 105, xiii, said to be in Columba's hand, which has also been traced in some parts of the well-known Book of Kells.

That transcription of the manuscript which was discovered at Kells, was done years later on Iona, after Columba had worked out his self-appointed task of winning as many souls for Christ as had been slain in the battle he had caused. When Columba left the shores of Ireland to complete that vow, he set out for a land long inhabited by his fellow countrymen. The Scots of Dalriada, a territory which more or less coincided with modern Argyll, were Irishmen who had crossed the narrow seas (it is only eleven miles from the coast of Ulster to the Mull of Kintyre) some time in the fifth century. The name of the land they settled comes from that of a tribe from County Antrim who claimed to come of a royal line. Fergus, the descendant of the river goddess Nes, was the mythical first ruler of the Scottish territory. He was succeeded by his more historical grandsons, Comgall and Gabran.

The Irish Scots brought their Christianity with them, but by the time Columba arrived they had lapsed from the faith, and it seems that he came to a land of warring, pagan tribes. Indeed, the real reason for his leaving Ireland in the first place could well have been to undertake a missionary journey to recall people to the true faith.

The date for Columba's arrival on Iona is given as 13 May 563, two years after he is supposed to have left Ireland. If these dates are correct, then somehow the time he spent on the journey has to be accounted for. This has been done by supposing that instead of making the long sea voyage through the islands to Mull and Iona, Columba sailed in the first instance direct to Kintyre.

There is a tradition that he landed near the present Southend village, at Keil Point to the east of Carskey Bay, pinpointed from a distance by the stark ruins of the technical college, destroyed in 1924 and oddly still left on the hillside. Below the modern ruin and a little to the west of it, on the island side of the road which runs along by the sandy stretch of the shore interspersed with the rocks from which herons fish, there is a series of deep caves in the pink rock of the hillside. Now they provide shelter for goats and sheep, but once people lived there. In the fourth century AD, when Kintyre was mainly inhabited by the Celtic Epidi, the tribe of the horse people, this was a thriving settlement whose people practised the craft of weaving and were visited by an itinerant smith, for the tools of both trades have been found here. It is very possible that these caves were still inhabited when Columba came here two hundred years later.

The church that is dedicated to him is a building of the thirteenth century. It stands a little to the east of the caves, and behind it is a pool almost covered by the surrounding Herb Robert and lichens. It is fed by the spring of St Columba's Well, whose waters are still used for Kintyre christenings. To the west is a small hillock on which stands a rock marked with footprints that are said to be Columba's. One is complete, the other is only half there, and together they give the unfortunate impression of two right feet. Between them someone has inscribed the date of 561 to show when the saint arrived in Scotland. Like almost every other visitor to the place, I put my foot where the saint is supposed to have trodden and that bore out the tradition that he was almost a giant of a man. The rock on which these footprints are marked could have been used as the socket for the twelfth- or thirteenth-century high cross, now in the museum at Campbeltown, and brought there from the rocky reef opposite the church, which is only accessible at high tide.

Dunaverty Castle

Beyond Southend's golf course, on pinnacles of rock jutting out towards Sanda Island, is the site – it is virtually no more than that – of Dunaverty Castle [68:685075], a stronghold which was held in the seventeenth century by the MacDonalds, and MacDougals against Leslie's Covenanting army. Dunaverty has a proud past. In the Middle Ages it was an almost impregnable fortress reached by a swaying bridge across turbulent waters, and marked the southernmost part of the dynasty, founded by Somerled, which ruled the Isles for three hundred years. Now it is approached through rough, deep sand and desolation, a wasteland whose misery is accentuated by the deserted hut put up to the memory of twenty-one-year-old John Ronald Ker, who was drowned here on 26 October 1867.

Campbeltown

The coast road to Campbeltown goes past a church dedicated to St Ninian and some caves where a six-armed variety of the Chi-Ro symbol at one entrance proves that an early Christian community lived here. These people could well have been visited by Columba on his journey north, but all we know for certain about them is that one of them, Kildusklend, was killed here in 617.

In the museum of the gently busy harbour town of Campbeltown the story is told of the way people lived in south Kintyre from the third millennium BC, and the sites of the Christian burial grounds on both east and west coasts are plotted. The town has a wide harbour with a sandspit, along which at low tide you can reach the conical island of Davaar, which boasts a painting of the Crucifixion in one of its caves.

North from Campbeltown the road to the east follows the coast, from which the traveller looks across the water to Arran. Columba must have gone north along this road or along the highway of the more level west coast where the A83 now runs, for both afford a much easier passage than the mountainous interior and both have been highways from prehistoric times. For today's traveller, the east-coast road, which is the minor one, has the prettiest settlements and villages. The A road goes directly by the sea with only rocks behind it; the B road with its little hump-back bridges is slower and gentler.

Here is Saddell and the ruins of its twelfth-century Cistercian abbey by the burn of Saddell Water, Allt na Monach or the monk's burn as it is called. The abbey is a burial ground now and Somerled himself lies here among the tombstones embossed with knights, in their *Leine chroich* (saffron-dyed quilted tunics) and pointed caps,

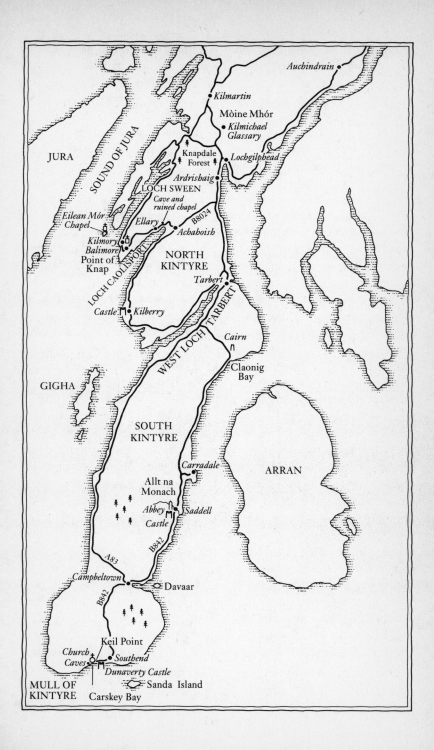

clutching their heavy claymores. A woman or child is also remembered here, and a priest whose chalice rests mysteriously above his solar plexus. Two of the grave slabs are marked with boats.

In summer it is a village of flowers, the cottage gardens divided by fuchsia hedges, but the oldest building dates from 1899. It stands on the roadside by the stream and a child's boot of a much earlier date was found in its foundations. Hence, its owner supposes (and with some reason) that there was at least one older building on the same site. The land of Saddell has long been owned by the Merton family, who once lived in a castle (now cared for by the Landmark Trust) which stands at the edge of Saddell Bay, a raised shingle beach forming a natural harbour, part of which is preserved as a wildlife sanctuary. Inland the road goes north through banks of rhododendrons to Carradace, birthplace of Professor Thom, the engineer turned prehistorian, and home of one of Scotland's best-loved writers, Naomi Mitchison.

Farther north at Claonaig Bay, from which a ferry runs to Arran in the summer months, the coastal road turns to the west. A couple of miles along this road, a chambered cairn stands on the hillside to the north [62:865583], facing east to the mountains of Arran. On the western side of the peninsula the road comes out by the little causewayed island from which the ferries go to Islay; and to the northeast of that is the narrow isthmus that joins North and South Kintyre.

It is very likely that Columba and his followers could have carried their coracles across this neck of land. In 1093, Magnus Barelegs, king of Norway, was promised by Malcolm III that he could have any island he could reach by ship with the rudder in place. So his men dragged his longship across the isthmus of Tarbert and so claimed the whole of South Kintyre, holding it for the Norse until they were defeated by Somerled on 6 January 1156. Three centuries later, the galleys of Robert the Bruce (who had a castle at Tarbert), together with those of Angus of the Isles, Lord of Kintyre, were dragged overland to sail south for a surprise attack on the MacDougall of Gigha. Although these war galleys were presumably heavier than most boats used for such journeys, the custom of dragging craft across the isthmus went on until the building of the Crinan Canal in the eighteenth century.

The minor road to the west, along the shore of West Loch Tarbert, goes to Kilberry, facing the Sound of Jura, where there is another collection of medieval grave slabs as well as some early plain crosses collected by the grandfather of Marion Campbell, Argyll's historian.

The present church of Kilberry dates from 1821, but it stands on the site of the twelfth-century church by Kilberry Castle. It is a place which was settled long before that, and the stones of very much earlier buildings and monuments have found their way into the thresholds and walls of the farm buildings on the 500-acre estate.

The next inlet is Loch Cáolisport, and a lane from the head of it at Achahoish runs along its northwestern shore to the little bay to the north of Ellary [62:748768]. The Rogers who own this land, and who have made a garden set with Peruvian lilies in the ruins of the twelfth-century chapel by the bay, have taken special care of the two caves, which were places of worship and burial for much earlier generations of Christians. The outer cave has an altar with a cross carved in stone above it, while near the entrance there is a shallow rock basin which could have been used as a holy water stoop or for the washing of feet. Excavations here have revealed tiny stone coffins, with the bodies all pointing towards the east. There is no doubt that those were Christian burials and that the caves were sacred places; nor is there any doubt that generations of fishermen used them as shelter. People were living in Jura's caves until the beginning of this century, and long before that burial parties from Jura sheltered in the caves as they took the bodies of noble dead to Iona.

Perhaps Columba landed at Ellary and not at Southend, for the current could well have taken him this far north. From Ellary, a path, along which some people have foolishly and unsuccessfully attempted to drive, goes round the hills to the rocky far-western shore and the two cottages that mark Balimore and the start of the road to Kilmory. That was a site dedicated to the seventh-century saint Mael Rubha, and marked now by the ruins of a thirteenth-century chapel [62:704753] in the middle of a collection of untidy farm buildings. The shell of the chapel is full of medieval grave slabs, some of which are marked with boats. They are all protected by a Perspex roof, which makes an uncanny sound in the slightest breeze of a summer day, and which must be absolutely eerie in wild weather. From the chapel, farm tracks run down to the shore, whence you can look across to the island of Eilean Mór. There, the ruins of another chapel mark it as a place of retreat for the holy men from the mainland settlement.

The road that follows the shore of Loch Sween goes past the holiday chalets in the grounds of the ruins of Castle Sween, and on through Knapdale Forest to the western end of the Crinan Canal which runs east to Ardrishaig, and makes possible a sea passage from Jura to Lochgilphead. The canal was subscribed in 1743 and built by James Watt, John Rennie and Thomas Telford eighty years before the Caledonian Canal was made.

From that evidence of the start of the technological age, we are brought back into prehistory by the Mòine Mhór, the great moss which lies to the north of the canal. This plain, bisected by the meanderings of the River Add and dominated by the rock of Dunadd, capital of the kingdom of Dalriada, was a place of religious significance in the Bronze Age.

Dunadd

The rock of Dunadd, rearing out of the marshes, was an Iron Age fort long before it was established as the main court of King Connel. It is still a majestic place. On one of my ascents, I was guided and escorted to the summit by a cheerful brown and white dog belonging to the farm at its base, who seems to have appointed himself a voluntary custodian. The massive entrance to the fort faces the southwest, and from here a modest climb earns you a supreme view and an entrance to a past world. The rock is on two levels, and there are still signs of a wall between the outer and inner fortifications. Near the pinnacle there is a stone bearing three marks: a right footprint, much smaller than the one at Kintyre, the faint outline of an inscribed Pictish boar and a small rock basin. This stone is a replica, a slab of a much lighter colour than the surrounding rocks, the original one having been removed for protection.

The Stone of Scone

The history of another stone, the Stone of Scone, which is commonly believed to have originated here, is altogether a more complex matter. The story goes that when Fergus, the first king of Dalriada, was crowned here in AD 500, making the first footprint in the Dunadd stone, he also brought with him the Stone of Destiny, which was no less than Jacob's pillow. This was set beside a magic cauldron which always supplied exactly the right amount of food for the number of people needing sustenance. In that tradition Christianity and paganism mingle, but the probable fact is stranger. It seems very likely

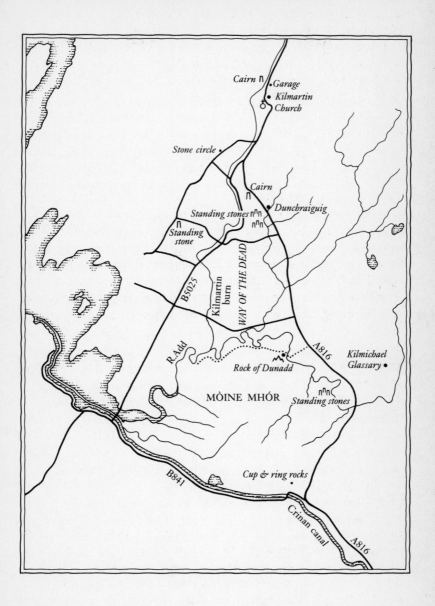

Cairn

Garage

Kilmartin
Church

Stone circle

Cairn

Standing stones

Dunchraiguig

Standing
stone

B5025

Kilmartin
burn

WAY OF THE DEAD

R.Add

A816

Kilmichael
Glassary

Rock of Dunadd

MÒINE MHÓR

Standing stones

Cup & ring rocks

B841

Crinan canal

A816

from excavations carried out in Dunsinane near Scone in the early nineteenth century that the original stone was actually Columba's portable altar, which he used at the coronation of Aidan. Compared to that, the block of old red sandstone now at Westminster is a matter of small significance.

The road that crosses the great moss now leads to Kilmartin at the head of the valley, flanked to the east by the mountainous region of Kilmichael Glassary. The road runs through the ominous Bronze Age Way of the Dead, marked out by cup-and-ring-inscribed stones, many cairns and one massive stone circle. One of the cairns, Dunchraigaig [55:833968] is a massive stone-covered burial chamber in a small wood by the main road. To the south of it is a pattern of standing stones which could be part of a stone row running up to the entrance of another cairn.

Glebe Cairn [55:834989] to the west of Kilmartin church is reached by a field path starting beside a garage by the main road; and the stone circle, which stands on a slight ridge and stretches across two fields, is to the west of Kilmartin Burn [55:825978]. The evidence of the early Christian settlement in this area is to be found in the eighth-century cross preserved among the grave slabs in Kilmartin church, and in the 'shrine' discovered in 1814 by workmen clearing a stone wall round the nearby church of Kilmichael Glassary [55:859934]. This bronze 'shrine' was a form of reliquary, made to protect an iron handbell supposed to have been used by Columba's friend Moluag, who founded the monastery on Lismore. The 'shrine' itself, which is now in the National Museum of Antiquities in Edinburgh, is of twelfth-century design with a stylized Crucifixion embossed on one side of it. The seventh-century bell which it protected was wrapped in a red cloth, and the devout were able to touch it through a small hole in the metal plate that sealed the bottom of the cover.

From Kilmichael Glassary, whose name refers to the rich grazing lands around the village, a gated road, which starts off by a series of standing stones, winds for seven miles across the mountains to Loch Ederline and the main road to Ford at the head of Loch Awe. An older drove route leaves the mountain road at 55:875957 and goes northeast through the forest to Carron [55:945995], where it turns due north through craggy rocks and a string of little lochs, reaching the long Loch Awe after it has passed the ruins of Kilneuair church

[55:889038], which is dedicated to St Columba and which was once the site of the chief market in the district. Its ruin is now surrounded by yews and pines.

The easiest way to get to the ruined church is to approach it along the B840 from Ford. There is a footpath sign at the edge of the forest about two and a half miles from the village at 55:885038. If you go a few hundred yards along that track, you will come to the wall around the ruins, which stand at the edge of the wood on a slight mound overgrown with bracken.

There are steps over the wall, and inside the enclosure a fairly clear entrance path leads to a group of worked stones by a small building full of nineteenth-century burials. From here, if you want a good twelve-mile walk to the south, you can follow the drove as far as Carron, and then take the more defined track running northeast to Loch Fyne and the museum of farming life at Auchindrain, founded by Marion Campbell on the site of a township that was a going concern until the beginning of this century.

Loch Awe

Although I shall return to Loch Awe in the next chapter, which follows the routes that the latter pilgrims took to Iona, and although any traveller to the north, in any age, would obviously take the route through the mountains and along the narrow coastal plain now followed by the A816, it is worth going the long way round to reach Kilmelford by following the difficult minor road along the northern shore of Loch Awe and that of the tiny Loch Avich. Halfway along the Loch Awe road at Kilmaha [55:942084] there was a Christian cell; its dedication is uncertain but it is of an age to mark the place where one of Columba's followers made his solitary retreat.

From Kilmelford the main road goes towards Oban and the turning west to Easdale, but it is possible to take the minor road to Melfort and then to walk by the shore of the loch, cutting inland from Kilchoan Bay to cross the peninsula to Ardmaddy Bay [55:786161] and so join the road that crosses the bridge over the Atlantic to Seil Island and the old slate mining village of Easdale. It was here that the film of Gavin Maxwell's *Ring of Bright Water* was made; the backdrop of immaculate holiday cottages, their neat gardens walled with the indigenous slate, makes the place still look like a stage set.

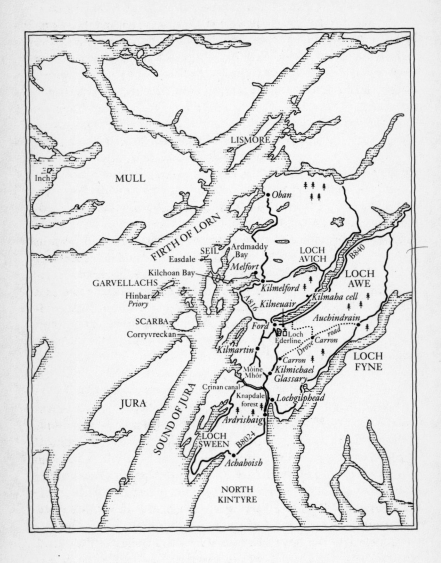

LISMORE

MULL

Inch

Oban

FIRTH OF LORN

SEIL
Ardmaddy
Bay
Easdale
Melfort

LOCH
AVICH

B840

Kilchoan Bay

GARVELLACHS

Kilmelford

LOCH
AWE

Hinbar
Priory

A816

Kilneuair

Kilmaha cell

SCARBA

Ford

Auchindrain

Corryvreckan

Loch
Ederline

Carron road

Kilmartin

Drove

Carron

*Kilmichael
Glassary*

LOCH
FYNE

*Môine
Mhôr*

Crinan canal

JURA

SOUND OF JURA

Knapdale
forest

Lochgilphead

Ardrishaig

*LOCH
SWEEN*

B8024

Achahoish

NORTH
KINTYRE

In the early Middle Ages it was slate from Easdale that was used to roof the new abbey of Iona. Quarrying went on here until the nineteenth century. It came to an abrupt end. Nine years after a large community hall had been built to serve the quarrymen and their families, a freak storm on 22 November 1881 filled the quarries with water and the industrial village died. Now Easdale's economy is based on tourists, whose cars fill a vast park by the harbour. To leave them you can take a footpath up into the hills, and from the heights look west to the islands of the Garvellachs, the southernmost of which may have been Columba's own retreat of Hinba. If that was so, perhaps his intense affection for Hinba, to which no scholar has been able to give a confirmed location as yet, arose because it was from here in 563 that he finally set sail across the Firth of Lorn to Iona.

Another version of Columba's journey from Ireland to Iona ignores Kintyre, and would have him sail direct from Ulster to the little island of Oronsay. Those who hold that view claim that he would have settled there if he had not been able to see his homeland from its highest hill; for such was his yearning for Ireland and his repentance for the bloodshed he had caused there that he vowed never to set eyes on his homeland again. In fact he did return in 580, when he took part in the assembly at Druim-Cetta; and it is possible that the whole tradition of his ever coming to Oronsay was fostered by the monks of its medieval priory.

Iona

As for Iona, it had been a holy place for both Druids and Christians long before Columba landed there. In the fifth century the Druids are supposed to have come here to escape the persecutions of Imperial Rome, and to have founded a library on the island. In 410, when Fergus II of Scotland became an ally of Alaric the Goth, he added to that library by bringing back books from the plunder of Rome. So it was an established place of learning when Columba arrived. It is probably purely fortuitous that the island's name is the same as the Hebrew word for a dove. For centuries Iona was simply known as the Island, Eo, Hy, Hi or just I, which was expanded to Inis-nar-Druineah, 'the place of the Druids'.

More than twenty years before Columba came to Iona, a Christian cemetery was founded on the island by St Oran of Letteragh, who died in 548. This *Reilig Odhrain* was the burial place of the kings of Dalriada up to 560, three years before Columba's arrival. There is also a tradition that there was a college of seven bishops on the island at one time; and that two of them met the priest from Ireland and did their best to prevent him from landing.

Whatever sort of community it was that Columba found when he came to Iona, it is certain that he felt he had to set about its reformation. His first task was to build a church, and a strange tale is told about its building. It tells how St Oran sacrificed himself to the new church to the extent of actually being buried alive in the walls. To my mind that is partly a symbol for the way Columba's church was raised on an earlier foundation, and partly a reminder of the superstitious belief, common to many cultures, that makes the fortune of any building dependent on a sacrificial victim being immured in it during its construction.

It is that belief which accounts for the mummified bodies of cats that have sometimes been found in the chimney-breasts of old buildings in England; and probably indeed for the skeleton of the horse that was excavated from an earthwork in Iona itself. From what we know of the kindly good sense of Columba, it seems difficult to imagine that he would subscribe to such a cruel and pagan practice. It takes the imagination of a novelist like Eona K. McNicholl to suggest any literal solution to the persistence of the tradition that Columba's church was built on Oran's body. The Oran in her novel, *Lamp in a High Wind*, is not the saint of Latteragh, but one of a group of young men living in the decadent Iona to which Columba came. He saw the Irishman as the saviour of his beloved island, and chose to be the victim of a ritual murder carried out by his misguided friends to ensure that the saint's project would be blessed.

The mount which marks the place where Columba built his church still attracts a flight of white doves. It is a little to the north of the present cathedral, built by George Macleod in the 1930s on the ruins of the abbey founded by Somerled of the Isles in 1203. Now it houses the Iona community, whose members regard this island in some measure as Columba regarded Hinba, finding in it a place of retreat which enables them to gather the strength to carry out their work for peace and justice in inner-city areas. Yet they cannot experience the isolation which Columba found in his retreats, for in summer there is usually a youth group in residence, and although the number of day

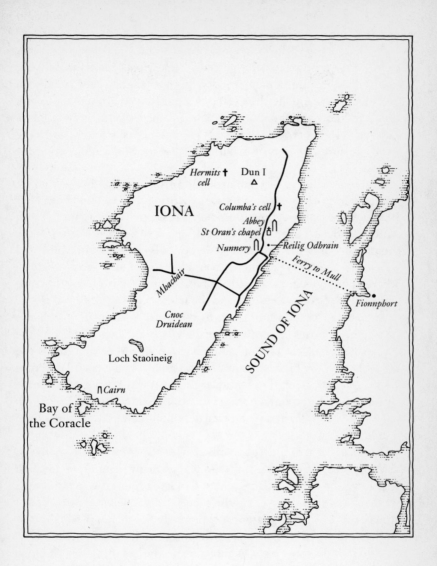

Hermits
cell

Dun I

IONA

Columba's cell

Abbey

St Oran's chapel

Nunnery

Reilig Odhrain

Ferry to Mull

Fionnphort

Mbachair

Cnoc
Druidean

SOUND OF IONA

Loch Staoineig

Cairn

Bay of
the Coracle

visitors has declined since the 1950s, about a hundred thousand people come to Iona each year.

Ian Galloway, a former warden of the community, claims that Columba was an active saint, and that 'Christianity is about walking rather than talking, about experiencing rather than discussing'. To demonstrate this belief he arranges a pilgrimage around the island each Wednesday. For a visitor with little time to spare on Iona this is quite the best way of seeing places that are not easily found, but there is no pleasure like that of making the discovery of a hidden site for yourself.

However you make your exploration of the island, you will be bound to start off, as all tourists do, by visiting the cathedral which has beckoned you throughout the short crossing from Fionnphort on Mull. Beside it is St Oran's Chapel, and a little inland from it the mound of Columba's cell, and to the south is the site of his tomb and the *Reilig Odhrain*, the ancient burial place of the Scottish kings, where one Englishman, Ecgfrid of Northumbria, lies among the royal tombs of the Scots, the Norse and the Irish.

Across the island's one road, to the north of the site where the community houses its youth camp, there is an earthwork marking the place where Columba's monks met in council, and behind that is the hill of Dùn I, the highest point of the island. If you head inland from there, keeping Dùn I to your right, you will come after some searching to the site of a hermit's cell outlined by a low circular wall some 18 feet in diameter, and probably built and used by one of the Culdees of Iona.

It is possible that the Abbot Cillen, who was an anchorite, managed the affairs of the abbey from this site; but many people like to think that it was one of the places where Columba himself went to pray. I was led to the place by seeing the superficially much more impressive stones of a considerably later cattle pound in the shelter of a high rock.

From the hermit's cell, you are bound to be tempted to climb Dùn I. Indeed, if you only have a short time on the island, this is what you must do first, for it is from here that you can best delight in the contrasts of its silver sands and translucent green seas pinpointed with a scatter of rocks and small islands.

On the northern brow of the hill is the Well of Youth, a reedy swamp in a green isolated glade among the rocks. From there looking southwest, you will see the greensward of the Machair, the stretch of grazing land that runs down to the western sea, and which is cut off from the southern coast of Iona by a steep ridge, Cnoc Druidean. Some will tell you that hill still holds the memories of cruel Druidic practices, and that it is the only dark place on the island.

A muddy and rutted track climbs up to it from the Machair and brings you through a rocky passage to the little loch which now provides the island's water supply. From here a gloomy path descends to the Bay of the Coracle, where Columba first landed. Above it is the Cairn-of-the-Back-to-Ireland, which he is said to have raised when he decided to settle here.

This part of Iona's coast has strong currents that make it unsafe for swimming, but the shoreline offers even more to the explorer than can be found among the rocks rising from the white sands of the north. Here is the long-disused medieval marble quarry where beautiful translucent green stones can be found. If you start off by following the old quarry road and go northeast from here you will come to a wide sheltered camping place between sea and rocks overlooking the island of Erraid.

The inland road running north through the cultivated fields takes you back to the cathedral past the island's present school and the ruins of the medieval nunnery, first ruled by Somerled's daughter, Beatrix. She must have been aware of the little Sheela-na-Gig, an obvious and rather charming pagan fertility symbol above a window on the outer wall of the nunnery, set there at least six hundred years after Columba had established his firmly celibate community on Iona.

✝

CHAPTER FOUR

From Iona to the Picts of the Northeast

Our knowledge of Columba's life on Iona comes from Adomnan, who became abbot to the community in 679, eighty years or so after Columba's death. He wrote the life of his saintly predecessor and tells us that in his latter years Columba had the face of an angel. Moreover, 'He was of excellent nature, polished in speech, holy in deed, great in counsel . . . a single one of his labours would seem beyond the powers of man. And in the midst of his toils he appeared loving unto all, serene and holy, rejoicing in the joy of the Holy Spirit in his inmost heart.' As for his way of life, he was a vegetarian and neither drank ale nor took condiments with his food.

He took the flower of the wild Saint John's wort, which grows plentifully on Iona, as his emblem, because it was named for his favourite saint; and as he was supposed to have carried bunches of it with him wherever he went, the plant came to be called 'the armpit package of St Columba'. As such it was celebrated for centuries in Gaelic verse throughout the Western Highlands. This quatrain in its praise was translated by George Macleod from one of six poems, included in the nineteenth-century collection *Carmina Gaedelica* by Alexander Carmichael:

> *Its reward is better beneath my arm*
> *Than a jostling group of calving kine;*
> *Better the reward of its virtues' charm*
> *Than a herd of cattle white a-shine.*

The comparison with the prized herds is significant, for Columba was to become the patron of cattle; like so many of his holy contemporaries he was a lover of animals and had a special affinity with them. Stories about his relationship with beasts extend from his refusal to bless a butcher's knife to his rescue of a storm-battered crane that flew to Iona's shores.

The impression of the Iona community under his rule is one of simplicity and peace. An Irishman was brought across the sea to tend his gardens and, according to Bede, the island was able to provide enough food to sustain five families. Yet it was not families, but a group of monks who lived off the produce and had a sufficiency for their many visitors. They dressed in cowls, white tunics and sandals, and the rule they followed demanded obedience, celibacy, poverty, caution and reason in speech, humility, hospitality and kindness to animals. They fasted every Wednesday and Friday apart from those weeks which fall between Easter and Whitsun. During Lent no meat was eaten until the evening. The laws of hospitality overruled the ritual fasts, however – when guests were among them they ate with them, returning to their own regime with renewed austerity when they were on their own. What milk and butter they had must have come from Mull if the story is true that Columba would allow no cows on Iona, claiming that wherever there were cows there were women, and wherever there were women there was trouble.

King Brude

The real threat to the peace of Iona in the early years of Columba's settlement came not from women, but from the Picts. For their high king, Brude, who ruled Alba from modern Inverness, had extended his territory into Dalriada; and the island which Columba had settled with the blessing of King Connel from Dunadd could be taken from him at any time.

It was probably this uneasiness as much as any missionary zeal that prompted Columba to confront the Pictish threat, and to undertake the long journey through the Great Glen to Brude's palace. Much of his journey would have been made in light boats, which could be carried overland between the lochs. The dangers would come from the uninhabited mountain wildernesses between the water, the forest home of bears, boars, wildcats and wolves. Today you can make the whole journey by boat through the Caledonian Canal, and the only hazards on the roads in summer come from the traffic. But anyone who leaves the main highways will come across wild enough areas, and even some signs that Columba and his followers passed this way.

According to Bede, Brude was converted to Christianity in 565 and confirmed Columba's rights to Iona at the same time. If that is so, the saint must have set out on his journey in the third summer after he settled on the island. He would not have gone alone. The names of two people have been suggested as his companions on the journey: Comgall, the first abbot of Bangor in Northern Ireland, and Kenneth, another Irish abbot, whose further journeys in Scotland we shall follow in the next chapter.

It would seem likely that Columba would have started off by sailing from Iona to the island of Lismore, where his friend Moluag had his settlement, and then continued by water to the head of Loch Linnhe, where Fort William is now. At any rate the Free Church in that sprawling and uninspiring tourist centre is built on an early Christian site.

Loch Lochy is the most westerly of the three lochs of the Great Glen, and there are several ways to reach it from Fort William. The first takes the B8004, which leaves the main road to Mallaig at Banavie, and goes along the west side of the Caledonian Canal to Gairlochy. Walkers will find the towpath on the opposite bank of the canal and it is pleasant enough to follow; but for a real hill walk, leave the B road where it crosses the river Loy [41:148818] and follow the minor road to Inverskilavulin [41:126834], and then make the trackless climb over the Beinn Bhàn mountains to Achnacarry and the head of Loch Arkaig. The alternative is to keep well to the southeast of the canal and set out towards Spean Bridge along the track which starts by the ruins of a tiny cluster of cottages opposite the pony trekking centre near Tomacharich [41:143783].

That walk is gently pleasant, a three-hour saunter with the head of Ben Nevis and Carn Bearg Dearg to your right, and the Great Glen cattle ranch immediately below you on the other side of a small stream fed by the waterfall which pours down towards the farm of Auchindaul halfway along the route. The track goes along the side of the hills to Highbridge, and from there you must join the main road.

From Clunes [41:204885] a forestry road runs above the north shore of Loch Lochy, coming down to the lochside by the ruins of Glas-Dhoire [34:253933], where there is a most convenient little bathing beach. If you want to do some more fairly tough hill walking, then go to the southwest of the loch and climb up past the waterfall of Glean Cia-aig [34:178894] and make a great semicircle over the hills to Allt Glas-Dhoire and the path which comes down through the conifers to join the forestry road at 34:252936. This road joins the shore road at Kilfinnan by the Laggan Locks.

The next stretch of water through the Great Glen is little Loch Oich, and the main road follows its northwestern shore to Invergarry. Here you will find more traces of Charles Stuart and the havoc that followed the 1745 rebellion than of the saints who journeyed here over a thousand years before. By the side of the loch, in the grounds of Glengarry Hotel, are the ruins of Invergarry Castle [34:316007], once the stronghold of the MacDonnels and burned down by Butcher Cumberland in ravages of desecration and slaughter. If you want to walk the length of this loch, you can follow the path along the south-eastern shore from Laggan Swing Bridge to Aberchalder [34:343034].

Fort Augustus

From the bridge of Oich at the head of the loch, you can either take the main road or walk by the Caledonian Canal, descending into Fort Augustus beside its four steep locks. Apart from St Benedict's Abbey, a nineteenth-century building housing a boy's school, Fort Augustus has now become almost entirely a tourist town, and although it is a good centre for walks in itself it has little to detain you.

Before General Wade established the place, as a military post, it was known as Kilcumin, in memory of the cell founded here by Cummine, abbot of Iona from 657 to 669 and author of the first life of Columba. Now the whole life of the town seems to be centred on the locks of the Caledonian Canal and the swing bridge which divides them from Loch Ness.

Despite the treacherous currents and tunnelled winds of that stretch of water, there is no doubt that Columba, who is said to have braved the whirlpool of Corryvreckan to the north of Jura, would have sailed the length of it. However, he would not have ignored the people on its banks, and there are signs of his passage and that of several other early saints on both sides of the loch. In fact, they are so numerous that the whole of the Great Glen is also known as the Valley of the Saints.

The main road goes along the north shore of Loch Ness, and bends inland to go past a waterfall which streams down from the mountains where the River Moriston flows into the loch. If you are motoring along this road, and nobody could want to walk here, it is worth stopping at the cluster of houses that make up Invermoriston and go into

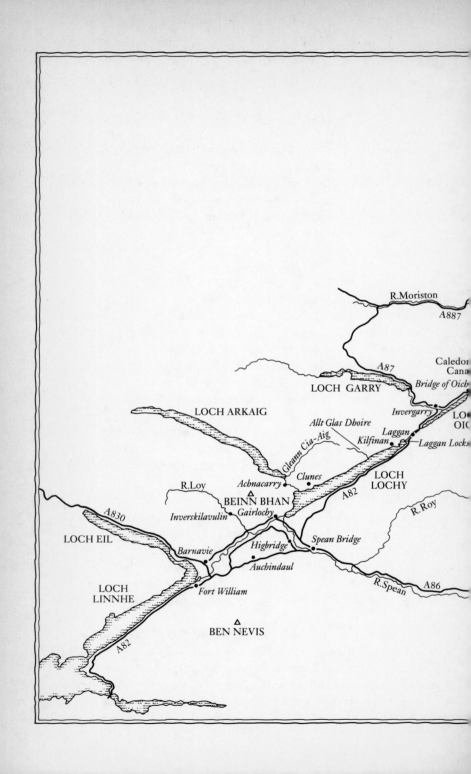

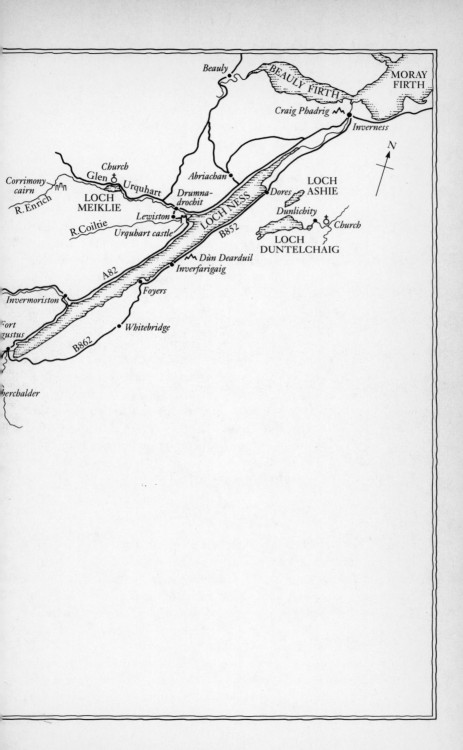

Falls Wood to the east of the main road [34:423165]. The path through the beech trees, which rise from a carpet of wood anemones, leads to a hexagonal stone gazebo above the waterfall. One of its windows frames the high stone arches of the two bridges over the old and new roads which cross the river as it runs into Loch Ness.

To the north, an oval-shaped burial ground by the main road is supposed to be set on the site where the fifth-century Pictish Saint Mercheird founded his church. Like many another saint, he left the selection of a site to divine guidance, stopping at that place where his handbell rang of its own accord for the third time.

The next inlet on this side of the loch occurs where the waters of the Coiltie and the Enrich converge at Urquhart Bay by Drumnadrochit. On the south side of the bay are the massive ruins of the castle of Urquhart, destroyed in the Jacobite uprising of 1689. That castle replaced many earlier buildings on the same rocky eminence, one of which is said to have been a monastery founded by Columba.

Whether that is so or not, there is plenty of evidence that in the wooded and fertile valley of Glen Urquhart Christian cells were established and that, as we have seen, some of them date from the time of Ninian. There is even a local belief that one of the trees under which the saint sat was still growing when the road at Temple by the shores of Loch Ness [26:520300] had to be widened in the 1930s. That belief was so strong that when the tree had to be felled so that the road could run through no Scot would cut it down, and an Englishman had to be brought in to do the deed.

Glen Urquhart

Long before the Christians came, the Picts inhabited this glen, and even gave it its name, for Urquhart is one of the few Pictish words that remain. It means 'woodland'. Unlike most stretches of the Highlands which were so severely eroded at the time of the clearances, much of Glen Urquhart still remains wooded. It is a glen surrounded on all sides by mountains, which one of its inhabitants, Mrs Hugh MacDonald, likens to the waves of the sea.

She has lived for many years in one of the houses that line the single road of Lewiston at the entrance to the glen. Her husband was a keeper of ancient monuments, and in his retirement he took it upon himself to work on the restoration of the Bronze Age chambered cairn at Corrimony [26:385304]. It is at the head of the glen surrounded by twelve stones, and served both as a burial place and a temple dwelling. The entrance faces southwest and leads to a small passageway opening into a rounded chamber which could have been used for both burials and religious rites. Mrs MacDonald told me of the popular belief that the passageway to the cairn was made small enough to let in the Druids, people of tiny stature to her way of thinking, while preventing wild beasts from pushing their way in. She had also heard that the cup marks on the capstone were designed to be filled with the blood of lambs sacrificed to the sun.

At Drumnadrochit, the old chapel of St Mary by the lochside [26:515295] is supposed to be set on the site of a cell founded by Drostan, one of Columba's dearest friends and companions. Now the place is submerged by the dead from the seventeenth century to the present day. They lie so thick here that it is almost unbearable to walk to the ruined ivy-covered walls of the chapel in the midst of the graves.

By the side of the main road going along the lochside to Inverness there is a nursery garden specializing in heathers. Just beyond it is another ruined church [26:572346]. It also stands on a place that has held a Christian building since the sixth century. Its churchyard, which includes a fourteenth-century grave slab, is planted with Lawson's cypress, which make it visible from the opposite shores of the loch. Above the church, in a little oak grove, there is a cluster of stones. The sturdy central one is substantially indented, and is known as St Columba's font, for it holds water in even the driest summers. It seems a natural place for baptisms and they used to take place here, but the 'font' is most probably a hole for the post which once supported the roof of a monastic cell. When I went to see this place, the brown lop-eared goats (belonging to Dr and Mrs Mungo who own the nursery garden) stood around the glade giving the place an oddly biblical flavour.

If you continue along the path through the wood, you will come to the steep lane which joins the village of Abriachan to the lochside. This is the home of Mrs Katherine Stewart, writer, museum curator and sub-postmistress. The museum of crofting implements and history which she collected is housed near the old schoolhouse where she lives. From there a lane goes west towards the main road that links Beauly and Drumnadrochit. Where the lane meets the road you will find the ruins of the church of Convinth [26:512376], a name that comes from the Pictish *coin-me* (waiting upon a visiting lord). The church ruins stand on a little knoll, and long before it was built there was probably a Celtic monastery here, which may have been known to the St Conngan to whom the later church was dedicated. He was an eighth-century Irish chieftain, who was exiled in Scotland like Columba. His nephew, St Fillan, arranged for his body to be buried on Iona.

The churchyard is planted with larch trees now, and it was around this site that a massive, annual fair was held up to the seventeenth century. People climbed up to it from Glen Urquhart, and walked from the crofts which now stand in ruins on the way to Abriachan along lanes whose verges are bordered in summer with the delicate but sadly named sneezewort. From here you can look northwest to the perpetual snows of Easter Ross.

From Abriachan the road to Inverness goes through conifers and then past a Bronze Age hut settlement of eleven circular dwellings on the west side of Cnoc na h'Each draidie [26:550364]. The hillside has been left unplanted by the Forestry Commission, so you can walk through the heather and find the stones that were used over three thousand years ago to build the village, which may have been abandoned by the time the Iron Age forts were established at the mouth of the Ness.

Inverness

No one quite knows the site of the high king's palace at Inverness where Columba confronted Brude. There are three possibilities: the castle hill which is now in the centre of the city and crowned by the modern administrative buildings; the Hill of Torrean, also well within the city limits; and the vitrified hill fort of Craig Phadrig, overlooking the Beauly Frith. Although the Hill of Torrean, where a silver chain, a common adornment of Pictish chieftains, was found, is the most likely candidate, it is still worthwhile climbing through the forestry drive to the fort of Craig Phadrig, with its massive puddingstone walls. On this site it is not easy to find the clinkers of vitrified stone, which show that, in common with many other Scottish Iron Age hill forts, the massive timbers in the stone walls had been set alight, either accidentally or as a way of welding the wall together. A paved entrance at the west end takes you into a large hilltop enclosure covered with a tangle of dog roses, willowherb and foxgloves.

Columba's first miracle in this stronghold of Druidism was actually to get into the place, by making the sign of the cross before the heavily barred and guarded gates, and to persist with his mission until he was able to speak with the king. There he found that the Arch-Druid Broichan was far more hostile than Brude, the high king; and most of the stories that have grown up about the miracles that took place during this visit of Columba to the Pictish capital concern the confrontation between the rival priests. One simply relates that when the Druid showed his power over nature by milking a bull, the priest responded by turning the milk into wine. Other stories tell of Columba's power in restoring a dead slave girl to life, in causing one of the Druidical healing stones to float, and in calming a storm on the turbulent waters of Loch Ness. Adomnan even relates a miracle which occurred when the saint encountered a beast, which some have taken to have been the prototype of the Loch Ness monster but which more probably represented the Druidical water horse, a dreaded *genus loci*. Whatever the creature was, Columba saved a man from being attacked by it with the simple rebuke, 'Thou shalt go no further, nor touch the man: go back with all speed.'

Brude, however, does not seem to have needed miracles to persuade him that Columba's faith was the true one. He became converted to Christianity, gave the saint security for his settlement on Iona, and arranged for his disciples to have safe conduct for their travels along the northeast coast to Orkney. Yet Brude's people seem to have been reluctant to support him, and after what must have been an uneasy reign he met his death in an inter-tribal battle.

Loch Ness

Meanwhile Columba must surely have returned as soon as he could to take the good news to Iona. In following his route back to the west, at least as far as Fort Augustus, I should like to look at the early Christian imprints along the southeastern shores of Loch Ness. For a long time that bank of the loch provided a better highway than the other, and it was along this route that General Wade built two of his famous military roads. One such has now been converted into the B862 from Inverness to the lochside village of Dores. A mile or so east of that road, a carefully protected Pictish stone engraved with Brude's insignia of a boar stands at the edge of a field by the lane to Knocknagael [26:657413]. To the west of General Wade's road is Aldourie Castle, which having been built in 1754, has nothing to do with the story of the saints, but whose grounds are worth visiting for the pleasantly wooded lochside walks that they provide, and as a small pilgrimage in honour of the Pre-Raphaelite painter, G. F. Watts, who came here in 1886 at the age of sixty-nine with his new wife, Mary Fraser Tytler, whose home this was.

Southeast of Dores the minor roads towards Strathnairn go round the head of Loch Duntelchaig, through a land of grey eroded heights and much evidence of Bronze Age settlement, to the church of Dunlichity [26:659330]. Although this is superficially a rather dull early-nineteenth-century church, it is made interesting in a macabre fashion by the watchtower at its gate set up to prevent the activities of Burke and Hare resurrectionists who could realize sixteen guineas from the medical schools for every corpse they made away with.

This church was build on the site of a late medieval church, which in turn replaced an even earlier one dedicated to St Finnian. Dunlichity seems to have been a natural place for religious activity. At about the time that the present church was being built, the outlawed Episcopalians were using a secret place on the moorland for their meetings, taking a hollowed boulder for a font.

The hills between Strathnairn and the Great Glen are full of many other strange and dramatic places, often seeming even more remote than they actually are. In the middle of a field behind a ruined farmstead near Midtown, there is a chambered cairn [26:623325] with an enormous capstone, which is well worth walking to. Nearby, the reverberations of a battle fought in the first century BC on the shores of Loch Ashie are still said to produce phantoms around the fort of Dùn Riabhachardi on Ashie Moor [26:601317]. One visitor actually thought he had a glimpse of a pageant, only to be told that nothing of that sort was going on.

Culloden

Similar ghostly echoes are told of the battle of Culloden, which took place on the hills some miles to the northeast. In the valley beneath that doomed moor are the majestic Stones of Clava, hidden in a glade among the cornfields. This was surely a site sacred to Broichan and his high priests, even though it was chosen by people who lived at least a millenium before them. Here you will find three passage graves beneath distinctive cairns, each one of which is surrounded by a circle of upright stones. The ones that have been excavated here are only a fraction of such monuments in this area.

General Wade's road from Dores continues along the lochside, crossing the new bridge at Inverfarigaig [26:523238]. Upstream from here, Columba's friend Moluag founded a church by the ford beneath the Pictish stronghold of Dùn Dearduil (Deirdre's Fort). The rickety decaying pier by the stony shores of the loch is a remnant of more recent history. Forty years ago it was one of the mooring stations for the waterbus that took farmers and their goods from one end of Loch Ness to another. Still affectionately known as the whisky route, the busride seems to have provided some happy outings.

From Foyers the road goes on towards Fort Augustus, flanked by the grey stretch of the Monadhliath Mountains to the left, and the loch waters hidden by steep banks of conifers to the right. There are several forest roads winding down to the lochside, where roe deer wander among the trees and the scrub of juniper bushes. The best route starts a couple of miles to the west of Wade's Whitebridge, through the lane to Knockie Lodge Hotel. It is a pleasant way to complete a journey through the Great Glen, walking the twisting path that brings you abruptly and almost unexpectedly to the waterside.

Nine years after Brude's conversion and Columba's return to Iona, Connel died and a new ruler of Dalriada had to be chosen. It was the Celtic practice, dictated by the necessity of avoiding a weak king, to ignore the random method of primogeniture, and to select the strongest and most suitable member of the royal family as the king's successor. In this case it was Columba, from the strength of his dual position of priest and statesman, who made the decision.

Aidan

He was in retreat on the island of Hinba when the news of Connel's death was brought to him. Whether Hinba was one of the Garvellachs, as seems most probable to me, or whether it was a remote part of Jura as some scholars claim, it was there that he was instructed by an angel to consecrate Aidan as the new king. Left to himself that would not have been Columba's choice – he preferred the brother; but as both Adomnan and his other biographer, Cuimine, relate, when he started to put his case to the heavenly messenger, the angel struck him so severely that he bore the marks of that blow for the rest of his life.

Perhaps it was because the choice of the king was not entirely to Columba's liking that he showed his authority and the supremacy of the Church over the State by making Aidan come to Iona for the consecration ceremony.

Deer

Columba lived on for another twenty years after Aidan's coronation, building up his community on Iona. During that time he returned at least once to Ireland, established a monastery on Skye, and no doubt made several more journeys to the northeast. In 580, when he was over sixty, he is said to have travelled with his disciple Drostan into modern Aberdeenshire, and to have founded a monastery thirty-five miles north of Aberdeen at Deer, a place which gets its name, so the story says, from the tears (in Gaelic *deara*) which the two men shed when the time came for them to part and for Columba to go back to Iona.

The account of the founding of the monastery, which may well be apocryphal, appears in Gaelic in The Book of Deer, which was transcribed in the twelfth century. The following translation was made for an edition of that manuscript for the Spalding Club in 1869. It tells how the place of Deer 'was pleasing to Columcille, because it was full of God's grace, and he asked of the mormaer to wit Bede that he should give it to him; and he did not give it; and a son took an illness after refusing the clerics, and he was nearly dead. After this the mormaer went to intreat the clerics that they should make prayer for the son that health should come to him . . . They made prayer and health came to him. After that Columcille gave that town to Drostan and blessed it, praying that "Whosoever should come against it, let him not be many-yeared or victorious." '

The Death of Columba

Columba himself was many-yeared when he went to his peaceful death in June 597. Admonan tells how he spent his last day journeying through Iona in a cart to tell the brethren of his departure. A horse he had been fond of sensed the coming parting, and in defiance of his companions Columba allowed the animal to grieve, explaining as Admonan put it that 'to this brute beast, devoid of reason, the Creator Himself has in some way manifestly made it known that its master is about to leave it'.

Columba's last act on earth was one of transcription. Before going into his church to die he penned the words of the thirty-fourth Psalm: 'They that seek the Lord shall not want any good thing.' Then, lying down before the altar in the church he had built, he gave up his spirit and was received into the bliss of heaven. But his companions were left to lament for, in the words of St Comgall, they cried, 'My soul friend has died and I am headless; you too are headless for a man without a soul friend is a body without a head.'

CHAPTER FIVE

From Strathspey to Applecross

Loch Laggan

Kenneth or Canice, the Irish abbot who went with Columba through the Great Glen to Brude's palace at Inverness, died at about the same time as his friend. From his sanctuary on the island of Inch Kenneth off the west coast of Mull, to the north of Iona, he made at least one other journey to the east. At the end of Loch Laggan on the southern slopes of the grey and forbidding Monadhliath Mountains he established a settlement which for a short while was to rival Iona.

In the waters of Loch Laggan, which have been so sadly tampered with, a coracle made of hides stretched on wooden frames is said to have been found. I cannot trace the discovery, but if the story is true, it is tempting to imagine that this was the vessel that brought Kenneth or one of his followers northeast through Loch Linnhe, from whose head they might have gone up Loch Lochy to the waters of the Spean. Then they might have rowed or sailed it up the broad Loch Laggan to the golden beaches that mark its end. A road runs along the north side of the loch now, and a footpath goes along the southern shore between the water and the conifer forest. From the southwest, the way to that path crosses the River Spean at 43:433830, by the derelict stumps of the drowned forest around Moy Lodge. From its mid-course, you can look across to the Island of the Kings [42:498874], which is still graced by the ruins of a castle supposed to have been built by Fergus himself. Nearer to the shore is the smaller Eilean nan Coin [42:503875], where the ancient kings of Scotland kept their hunting dogs. For this was the royal home and pleasure ground when the administrative capital of the country was at Dunkeld.

The royal associations were to continue. The many-towered Ardverikie House [42:507875] stands on a small promontory once known as the Hill of the Standard. Queen Victoria came here with

Albert in the August of 1847, and she was so enthralled by the beauty of the place that she had thought to make it her summer residence. However, Balmoral proved to be less plagued with mosquitoes, and so the Queen went east.

Kenneth's settlement was on a hill to the north above Kinloch Laggan, just below the present Aberarder Lodge [42:535896]. Like the majority of ancient church sites in Scotland, it is no more than a burial ground now, overlooked by two forbidding kennels that remind you of Lagganside's hunting past. Only when you climb up to one of the rocky outcrops and look out through the trees over the sands at the edge of the loch can you get any sense that this could have been the place that once was as much sought after as Iona as a goal for pilgrimage.

It is likely that those pilgrims, and indeed Kenneth himself, originally reached Loch Laggan from the southern end of Loch Ness, crossing the grey mass of the Monadhliath by the Corrieyairack Pass, which, as General Wade was to discover, is the only route from Fort Augustus to Speyside. That route starts from the lane to the west of the lowlands to the south of Loch Ness [34:376074]. It follows the course of Glen Tarff, going south along the old military road through the Corrieyairack Forest to join the valley of the Spey at Melgarve [34:464959]. From there a track leads to Garva Bridge and the lane to the iron bridge across the Spey at Laggan. In the grounds of the hotel which stands beside the A889 (once General Wade's road to the south) there is a ruined church [35:616938]. This is one building that did not become a burial ground; instead, for several years it housed Dr Isobel Grant's collection of material relating to Highland rural life and folkways.

Kingussie

Her eloquent reconstruction of the past is now more appropriately displayed a little farther to the east, in the partly open-air museum at Kingussie. That town, which has now become a ski resort and even manages to have a slightly Alpine air, is laid out with spacious and elegant precision. It was not always so. In 1812, Elizabeth Grant of nearby Rothiemurchus noted in her memoirs that it consisted of 'a few very untidy-looking slated stone houses each side of a road . . . a few white-walled houses here and there, a good many black turf huts,

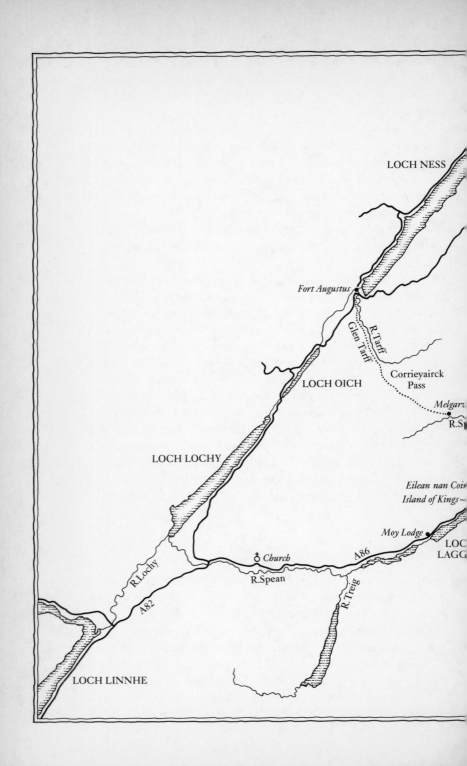

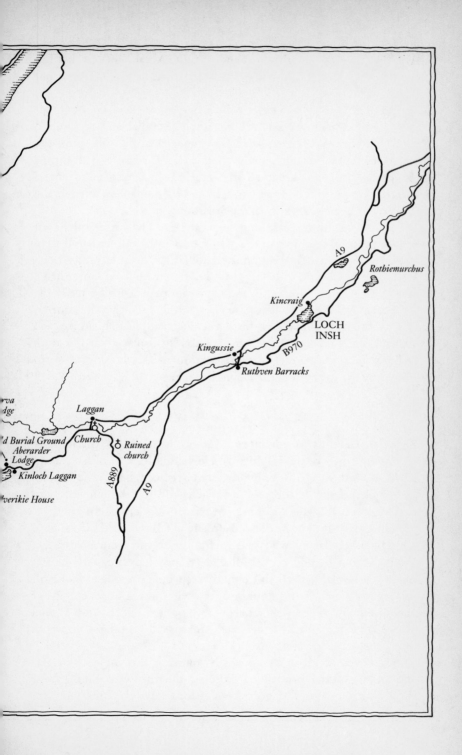

frightful without though warm and comfortable within'. Such a hut has been reconstructed in the grounds of the museum, and it bears out that description.

There can be no two more contrasting experiences than to enter that hut and then to walk a little way out of the town and climb up to the bleak Ruthven Barracks. These ruins crown the hill above the watermeadows of the Spey to the southeast of Kingussie. This formidable stronghold was occupied briefly in 1654 by Cromwell's General Monck. Wade extended the barracks in 1743, and they were finally destroyed twelve years later in the Stuart uprising.

The B970 running east along the south side of Strathspey arrives at a more peaceful reminder of the past: the seventh-century handbell in the tiny church at Kincraig on the knoll at the head of pretty Loch Insh. The bell is said to belong to Adomnan, who lived more than a hundred years after Kenneth, and whose journeys I shall trace in the next chapter. Wisely perhaps, the church offers the casual visitor no history or speculation about this slightly cracked, shapely bronze bell with its long, thin clapper, which is so proudly displayed on the south wall, flanked by two recently cast doves of peace. It hangs as a reminder of the strength of the Columban Church on Speyside.

The Isle of Mull

Kenneth belongs as much to Mull as he does to this totally contrasting area of the Highlands. He visited Iona from his cell on Inch Kenneth. It is now only inhabited by sheep, but in the Middle Ages a chapel served the people of the island and the pilgrims who came to the place where Kenneth began his wanderings. In 1773, Dr Johnson, sixty-four years old and already in failing health, came here with Boswell, daring wild seas in frail craft and riding bareback, often without benefit of a bridle. He responded so eagerly to the place that he claimed: 'Inch Kenneth is a proper prelude to Icolmkill (the cell of Columba). I doubt not but when there was a college at Inch Kenneth there was a hermitage upon Iona.' By the chapel founded by the Lord of the Isles, and already roofless, he wrote Latin verses to the saint.

The whole island of Mull is worth exploring. It is not just a road to hurry along on the way to Iona, although the thirty-seven miles from the landing stage of Craignure to the Iona ferry at Fionnphort are

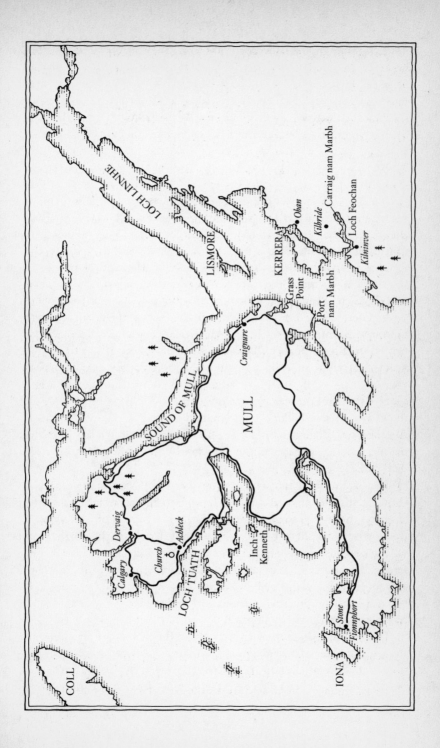

dramatic enough. The new road runs along the course of an old rutted highway, marked by standing stones, one of which is easily visible from the Iona bus at 48:314233. In parts this is a gentle route decorated by fuchsia bushes and little waterfalls; in others it is more sombre and challenging, with peat marshes and forbidding heights from which cascades fall through the crevices of the northern slopes.

Machar

Kenneth was not the only one of Columba's companions to have become familiar with the mountainous miles of Mull. Machar (whose friend Devenich is said to have preached the gospel as far north as Caithness) was one of the twelve who helped Columba found the settlement on Iona. When he was sent to the main island, he proved so successful in his missionary work and wrought such powerful miracles that the men of Iona grew jealous of him. So he was sent off across the Great Glen to join in the conversion of the Picts of the north and east. One tradition has it that it was Machar and not Drostan who first turned the Pictish fort at Old Deer into a monastery. It was there that he died, strengthened by a vision of St Martin, which was possibly prompted by a pilgrimage that he had made to Tours. A thousand years after his wanderings were done, the cattle drovers of Mars on their way to the Falkirk tryst greeted the sight of the church of Aberdeen as 'Eaglais na Machar', literally the church on the coastal plain, a pun on the name of the saint to whom Aberdeen's cathedral is dedicated.

The extent of the journeys of these early saints can be measured by the way that Machar of Mull is honoured in the northeast of the country, and by the small church dedicated to Ninian of Galloway on the northwest corner of Mull. You reach it best from the north-coast village of Dervaig, where the Old Byre Museum beautifully reconstructs the crofting life of the island in the nineteenth century. From that museum a four-mile hill road goes across the island to Torloisk. It is a route through lonely, dramatic hills where a double waterfall cascades down the rocky slopes.

The eighteenth-century church of St Ninian stands a few miles to the west on the coast road from Torloisk, on a site on which a church has stood since at least 1561, and which is generally thought to have been a place of early Christian settlement, owing its dedication to one of Ninian's missions. It stands on a slight hill overlooking the sea loch of Tuath. From here a footpath goes across the hills to Calgary. If you follow it, you will come out to the north of the bay which shelves up to a wide, sandy beach, and close to the path that leads to the ruins of the crofts deserted at the time of the clearances.

Moluag

The wild mountains of Mull are a great contrast to the sheltered, fruitful island of Lismore where Moluag made his base. It was from this comfortable place, whose name literally means 'the great garden', that Moluag and his followers took boat for Skye and then sailed across the Minch to Lewis. They also went as far east as possible, and Moluag established a cell at Rosemarkie above the Moray Firth on the Black Isle, whose green fertility, which belies its name, must have reminded them of their western island.

Strathpeffer

The way to the east took Moluag north of the Great Glen to the Pictish town of Strathpeffer. In the nineteenth century this place was to become an elegant Victorian spa, and its spacious, white hotels and wide tree-lined streets still testify to that splendour. It must have been a magnificent place in Moluag's day too, if the one Pictish remnant to be seen there now was typical of the whole. It is to be found in a field beside the red house opposite the entrance to the defunct railway station which has now been cleverly converted into an information centre and craft workrooms. In the field, which lies to the east of a narrow footpath, the stone stands on a little knoll. It is splendidly engraved with a triumphant and sophisticated eagle, crowned with one of the elaborate Pictish semicircles. Dealing with people who flourished under such proud emblems must have been a worthy challenge to the saint's wit and courage.

From the Black Isle, which was to be his second home, Moluag went to the Picts of the south, in the country to the north of Aberdeen. The church by the distillery at Mortlach by Dufftown, which still carries his dedication, stands on the site of the one he founded there in 566 as the centre for one of his largest monasteries.

Rosemarkie

Yet it was in the north that he died on 25 June 592, having returned to Rosemarkie on the Black Isle, a place that was to play an important part in Scottish church history for many centuries. It has now become a seaside town to the northeast of Fortrose, whose ruined cathedral dates from the thirteenth century. That cathedral was converted by David I from an earlier building which housed the Culdees of Rosemarkie, descendants of the religious who gathered around Moluag's cell. On Chanonry Point, the spit of land which juts out into the firth between the two towns, a cross bears evidence of the early Christian settlements here. A hundred years after Moluag's death, St Boniface, the missionary sent from Rome to draw the Celtic Church into the fold, died in this place. Despite his efforts, it was to be one of the last of the Culdee strongholds to abandon the practices of the Celtic Church.

Brendan

Men like Moluag may well have been inspired on their inland journeys by the example of Brendan, the Irish voyager, who is reputed to have visited Columba on the island of Hinba and, according to some traditions, actually founded the initial Christian settlement there. Brendan's voyages took him far across the ocean to the west, so there are few signs of his passage to be found in highland Scotland, but he is associated with Kilbrennan on the Isle of Arran, where he founded a monastery on the site of Kilpatrick.

While Brendan died in 575, Finbar, who was to become the patron saint of Barra in the Outer Hebrides, was a lad of fifteen and still studying in Ireland. Born in County Cork, the son of a metalworker and a slave girl, Finbar was to cross the sea to the east and found a monastery at Etargabail by the shore of Barra's Loch Gougane. Many students from his homeland were attracted there, and the place became a religious centre which was the focus for pilgrimages for centuries.

Dunblane

Blane, one of Finbar's contemporaries, is also associated with the islands, for he was born of a priestly family on Bute. After studying in Ireland, he returned to Scotland to become a priest and founded the monastery at Kingarth by the vitrified fort of Dunagoil on the island of his birth. He is, however, better remembered for his monastery at Dunblane, just to the north of Stirling. This city, which still bears his name, is graced with riverside walks beneath the present cathedral. They lead to a spacious green on which a pillar carries the quaint legend informing passers-by that, in 1849, Her Majesty's Commissioners gave a lease on 'this green yard of Dunblane as a bleaching green for the inhabitants'.

That nineteenth-century memento is most appropriate, for Dunblane's cathedral appeals to me as one of the finest and most sensitive pieces of Victorian restoration that I have come across anywhere in Britain. Here, beside the carefully preserved fifteenth-century choir stalls, stands a block of red sandstone reputed to be St Blane's preaching cross. The monastery which he founded was not placed beside the river, however. The beehive cells of Blane's settlement clustered at the top of the little hill to the east of the present cathedral, on the site of an old Pictish fort which defended the old road to the north. You can still see the remains of the stone walling which surrounded the original earthworks and marked out the summit enclosure, as well as the arch to the tunnel which led to the interior of the stronghold.

Donan

Despite their work amongst the warlike Picts, only one of Columba's followers who took the 'white martyrdom' of long wandering away from home met a martyr's death. This was Donan, an Irish monk of Iona, who founded his own monastery on the island of Eigg. In 618, he was burned to death with fifty of his companions when a gang of robbers, probably Vikings, attacked the church where the monks were celebrating the Easter mass. The pirates herded the bewildered priests into the refectory and set fire to it.

Eilean Donan

Churches dedicated to St Donan are found as far north as Sunderland, but most people will be more familiar with the island that bears his name than with any of the Donan churches, for it is reached by a footbridge from the much used road to the Kyle of Lochalsh where the Skye ferry starts. Eilean Donan, crowned with its restored medieval castle, must be one of the most photographed places in Scotland. It rises out of the waters at the place where Loch Duich meets Loch Alsh and Loch Long, and stands beneath the peaks of the Five Sisters of Kintail and in the shadow of the Cuillins to the west. It also was the site of a vitrified Pictish fort, on which Donan or one of his followers chose to establish a cell.

Near here, in 671, about seventy years after Columba's death, Maelrubha, one of his clansmen, a young Irish monk from County Down, crossed the water to the east. Two years later he established a group of beehive cells on the peninsula of Applecross, establishing a base on the island which has since become the Holy Isle of Eilean nan Naomh in Camasterach Bay. From here he explored the narrow coastal plain of the peninsula on which he was to establish his sanctuary.

Applecross

The un-Scottish sounding name of Applecross, which dates from a thirteenth-century document, is derived from Aber Crosam, 'the mouth of the river Crosam'. For centuries people simply knew the place as Comeraich, 'the sanctuary'; and that sounds far more suitable for this remote, enchanted place, surrounded by the bare rock of looming black mountains. It is as far removed from a cosy English village as anyone could possibly imagine.

There are now two overland ways of reaching the coast of this mountainous peninsula. There is the coastal road, built in 1977, which runs round its northern edge; and the ancient Bealach-na-Ba, the pass of the cattle, which climbs directly over the mountainous rocks of the heartland. I have found this to be the most dramatic drove road in Britain, and I had thought that the climb up to the Eppynt in mid-Wales was almost unbelievable.

The road to the rocky plateau above Applecross climbs from sea level to over 2000 feet in a stretch of six miles. Not surprisingly, it is a route forbidden to learner drivers, for its series of one-in-four hairpin bends are perched above precipitous cliffs. The summit provides one of the most breathtaking views of the Islands from Skye to the Outer Hebrides that I have encountered. Looking at all the surrounding

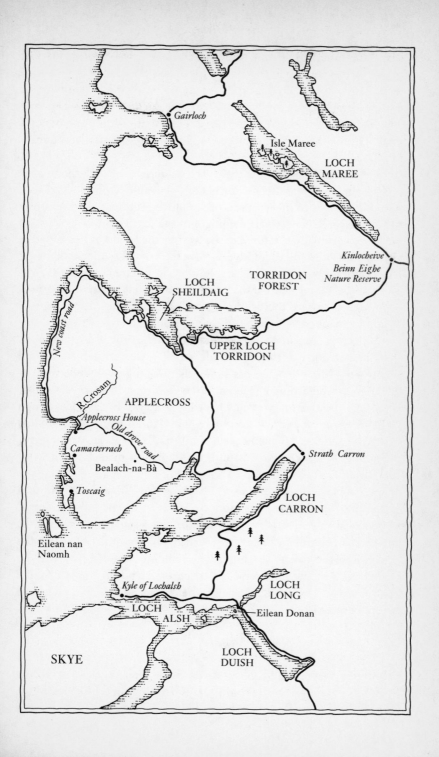

island mountains, I felt the same bewilderment that struck the poet Andrew Young alone in the face of the Cuillins. He could not decide 'whether they are angels met in an ecstasy of praise or devils conspiring against heaven'. Confronted by such awful grandeur, and still somewhat unnerved by the drive, I could not decide either, and I liked to think that if Maelrubha came this way he was similarly dumbfounded.

The distant peaks contrast with the wilderness of rock that makes up the immediate landscape of the high plateau of Applecross. From here the descent to the west is more gradual; even so, there are places where the road seems to be running into the sea. The people who live on the coastal plain, sheltered to the west by the Island of Raasay, were virtually on an island themselves before the coastal road was built, for the mountain road is only passable in good weather. From the post office at the western end of that road, the lane runs south to the bay of Camasterach where the fishing boats lie, and so on to the village of Toscaig to which boats from the Kyle of Lochalsh cross daily.

Applecross continued as a sanctuary from the time of Maelrubha to the Reformation. Within a six-mile arc of stones stretching around the estuary where Applecross House is now, fugitives from the law could find a breathing space and a chance to seek mercy for their cause. All the sanctuary stones have gone now. The last one, which took the form of an 8-foot-high cross at Camasterach, was smashed when the school was being rebuilt in 1872. There are varying reports as to whether that was pure accident or a piece of Protestant vandalism.

The abbey of Applecross was always associated with Bangor and not, as one might expect, with Iona, so it was appropriate that it should be mainly a base for Irish monks. Maelrubha set up his monastic cells and built his church by the estuary of the river Crosam, probably at the place where the kirk now stands. All his buildings were destroyed in the Viking raids of the ninth and tenth centuries and no traces of them remain today. The ruined chapel in the churchyard is of an uncertain but much later date.

Maelrubha

From this place, Maelrubha, whose name means 'the red priest' (perhaps on account of the colour of his hair) set out to the north. It is possible to follow him now, leaving the wide red sand of the beach which slopes gently into a translucent indigo sea, and driving along the new coast road, which rises and dips on its way to join the A896 to Loch Shieldaig. From its height you can look south to Skye and northwest across the Minch to the flat outline of Lewis and the shadowy hills of Harris, a panorama that is almost as splendid as the one from the rocky heights of the Bealach-na-Bà. Closer at hand are the roofless hulks of old crofts standing beside a few new cottages, whose inhabitants tend the tiny square fields, defined by stone walls, in the wider parts of this narrow coastal plain.

From Applecross the way to the north goes across the Torridon Forest from Upper Loch Torridon to Loch Maree, a place which attracted pilgrims to Maelrubha's shrine up to the seventeenth century. The name Torridon comes from the Gaelic *toirbheartan*, which means 'a place of transference', and there is a tradition that boats were once carried where the road now runs beneath the monstrous shapes of the ancient sandstone mountains, whose precipitous flanks are covered in swirling patterns of scree.

These mountains have been claimed as the oldest in the world; certainly there is no older range in Britain. Majestic and dominating as they are now, they are but a miniature of their former selves. Millions of years ago the high ridges that tower above the plain where the road winds its way were valley beds. On the sides of the rocks that are bare of scree, the flaky blues, greens and pinks of Lewisian gneiss, affectionately known as 'Old Boy' because of its extreme age, gleam in sunlight. Here and there, streamers of quartz, like icing on a wedding cake, adorn the rocky pinnacles.

Isle Maree

The road to the east of the mountains makes its way from the south to Kinlochewe, running past the Beinn Eighe Nature Reserve, which controls the passage to Maelrubha's Isle Maree [19:932724]. That little island lies off the roadless north shore of the loch, which takes its name from the saint. It is one of the loveliest of the larger lochs, the forests along its shores giving way to the bare rocks of the mountains, whose jagged ridges contrast with the flat slabs of the long islands, completely covered with all manner of broad-leaf trees as well as the inevitable pines, all of which have been growing here for at least nine thousand years. The road along the southern shore only passes one building, a hotel in which Queen Victoria stayed on 12 September 1877, when she visited Maelrubha's island. Now if you wish to visit the island you must make arrangements with the warden of the Nature Reserve, whose visitors' centre, open during the summer from 1 June, is at Anancaun by Kinlochewe [19:019630].

Isle Maree is one of the smallest of the islands in the loch, but it was a holy place to the Druids long before Maelrubha came to set up his own cell among their oak trees, which jostle for space and soil with ash, hazel, willow and birch, as well as the holly supposed to have been planted by the saint. In the centre of the little isle are the earthworks of his monastery, and the filled-in remnant of the well whose waters once transmitted healing to sick pilgrims. After Maelrubha's death pagan rites were re-established here in his name and bulls were sacrificed in his honour up to the seventeenth century.

We know from church records at Dingwall with what horror the latter-day Presbyterians viewed such goings-on; but it would be good to learn what Maelrubha himself felt about the way these Druidic practices were regrafted on to his own teachings. Such rituals, after all, are not far removed from the abundant and often outrageous tales of the miracles attributed to all the Dark Age saints by their hagiographers.

In worldly terms, Maelrubha certainly had great power. For fifty years, as abbot of Applecross, he virtually ruled all the territory to the north, travelling with his companions as far as Sutherland. It was there, at Skail in 722, that he died. He had reached the age of eighty.

His companions carried his body back across the wild mountains so that he might be buried at Applecross, at the heart of the sanctuary that he founded. Up to the time of the Reformation his grave was marked by a cross of red sandstone. Only two fragments of this have survived and they are to be found in the kirk, while the two round stones below the chapel in the churchyard are said to mark the place of his grave.

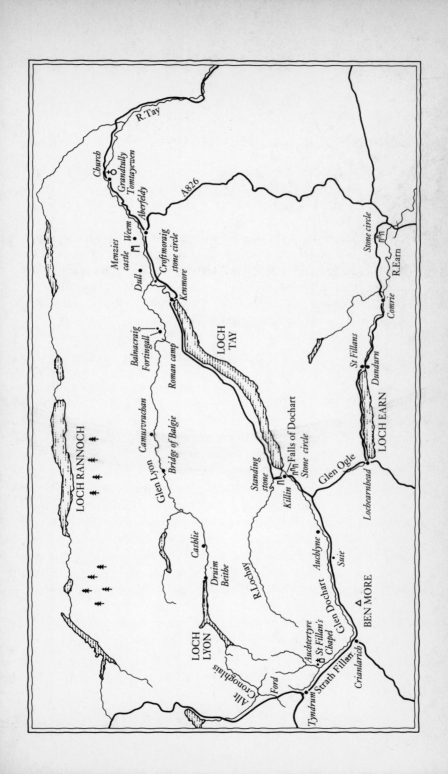

✝

CHAPTER SIX

Adomnan, Fillan and the Return to Iona

The handbell at the end of Loch Insh on Speyside is said to have been used by Adomnan, the seventh-century abbot of Iona, who wrote the first life of Columba, a glowing but scarcely credible account of his miracles and prophecies rather than a chronological biography. The siting of that bell proves that Adomnan himself was no laggardly traveller, but the main region to be associated with him lies to the south of it in the long and beautiful stretch of Glen Lyon.

Fortingall

Another of Adomnan's handbells can be seen at the entrance to that glen in the church of the estate village of Fortingall [51:743470], a slightly uneasy place despite its smart hotel and row of neat thatched cottages. The feeling of disquiet engendered by the miles of wire which firmly confine the traveller to the road does something to strengthen the tradition that Pontius Pilate was born here.

The story goes that the birth took place while his father was here on an ambassadorial mission, but as the Romans did not reach this part of Scotland until AD 84 the tale cannot carry much credence. Historical fact does not stop the earthworks just to the west of the village, commonly called the Roman Camp [51:735465], from being associated with the reign of King Metallanus, who ruled the Scots from Fortingall between 10 BC and AD 29. The king's palace is supposed to have been just to the west of Balnacraig Farmhouse [51/52:748474], and it was there that he is said to have received a Roman ambassador sent on a peaceful mission from Caesar Augustus. The story does not relate whether it was the ambassador himself or one of his staff who fell in love with the young Menzies girl, a close relation of the king, who became the mother of Christ's judge, born at the Roman camp in Glen Lyon.

That story apart, Fortingall should be a cheerful, healthy village. At any rate, by the end of the eighteenth century people here were living to a very great age. *The Statistical Account of Scotland* for the 1790s quotes a man and a woman living here who had each reached the age of 103, and thirty years before that, another inhabitant, Donald Cameron, achieved his 127th birthday. Even the yew tree in the churchyard is said to be the oldest in Britain. They claim it has survived three thousand winters. Certainly it was there when the plague victims were buried in the pit to the south of it, in the watermeadows by the river. And however exaggerated the claim for its age may be, it was also probably standing in the seventh century, when Adomnan worked among the sick and dying who succumbed to the pestilence that infected the glen in his time. Perhaps it was his courage and common sense that inspired the old lady of the fourteenth century who, with the aid of a single white horse to pull a sledge, undertook the burial of the plague victims by the river when there was no longer any room for them in the churchyard.

Milton Eonan

When Adomnan came to the glen from Iona he set up his cell and started a mill working near the present Bridge of Balgie, at a place which is still known as Milton Eonan, the mill town of Adomnan [51:571464]. He had been there some years when the plague struck, and the people who had come to love and trust him implored his help. The assistance he gave took the form of both divine intervention and common sense. Gathering his flock together at a hillock by Camusvrachan [51:621479], halfway along the length of the glen, he prayed with them and ordered the spirit of the pestilence to enter a nearby rock. A large hole appeared in the rock as the disease went through it into the depths of the earth. The rock can still be seen, and beside it is the stone slab marked with two crosses which the people of the glen placed there in gratitude for their deliverance. That they were spared to do so must be partly due to Adomnan's good sense in sending them away from the polluted waters of the river valleys into their summer huts, or shielings, on the surrounding mountain slopes.

It is fitting that the site of Adomnan's miracle should coincide with an even earlier holy stone, the Chriag Fhianaidh, or Stone of the Footprint. On top of the rock is the same sort of impression of a foot

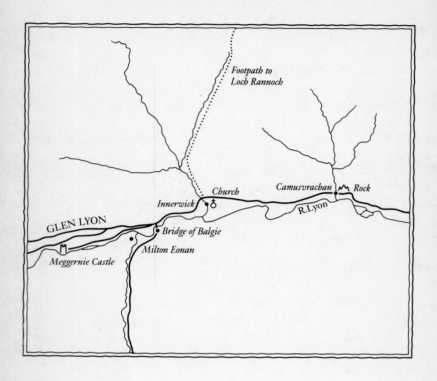

Footpath to
Loch Rannoch

Church

Camusvrachan   Rock

Innerwick

R.Lyon

GLEN LYON

Bridge of Balgie

Milton Eonan

Meggernie Castle

as we have seen at Dunadd and at Southend in Kintyre. No doubt it actually fulfilled a function in the installation of King Metallanus, although it has also become attached in legend to the fifth-century Saint Palladius, who, in historical fact, accompanied Germanus to Britain in order to try to quell the Pelagian heresy. Here in Glen Lyon he has become some sort of *deus loci*, and confused with the goblins or *urisks* who live in the burns.

Tyndrum

Adomnan is said to have come to Glen Lyon from Tyndrum [50:330304], which, in 1875, according to Queen Victoria's diary note for that year, was 'a wild picturesque and desolate place in a sort of wild glen with green hills rising around'. The old road that she travelled on has become the walkers' West Highland Way, and the trunk road, with a railway line on either hand, runs through a sort of tourist shanty town dominated by two hotels. The saint must have gone east from here to Loch Lyon, following the course of Allt Chonoghlais from the ford at 50:334359 to the headwaters of the loch. The mountains on either side of that arm of Loch Lyon fall steeply to the water, so we can imagine that Adomnan might have gone by boat as far as its head at Druim Beithe [51:444417] (although it is possible to walk along the side of the northern shore of the loch, where a footpath starts at 51:408420). From the end of the loch a lane goes beside the River Lyon to the present Bridge of Balgie, where he made his settlement.

The River Lyon follows such a winding course through rocky mountains that it has earned a Gaelic name signifying 'the crooked glen of stones'. The stones may, however, refer as much to the many ruined buildings along its banks as to the natural rocks. When Adomnan went east beside the river he passed the four Pictish strongholds at Cashlie [51:490419]. These forts or brochs were originally some 50 feet in height, and in places their walls reached a thickness of 25 feet. Over the years they have been destroyed, their stones used for other purposes, and the only sign that they existed lies in a few pieces of rock and masonry and some low grassed-over walls.

Meggernie Castle is in much better shape. Its square tower [51:554460] was built in 1582. This castle, which is still a private residence, was enlarged to its present size a hundred years later. That enterprise had to be financed by the sale of the part of the ancient wood of Caledon that made up the forest of Glen Lyon. The merchant who bought the land burned what timber he could not use, thereby so choking the river that no fish could live in it, and robbing the people of their winter fuel.

A mile or so from Adomnan's mill town another saint is remembered by the handbell which hangs in the church porch at Innerwick [51:588475]. It is said to have belonged to St Cedd, brother of Chad, the founder of a monastery where Lichfield Cathedral now stands. Both brothers were educated at Lindisfarne by Aidan, and although Chad is mostly known for his work amongst the East Saxons, he frequently returned to the north. Overshadowed by his more powerful brother, Cedd himself was successful enough in his missionary journeys for Finan of Lindisfarne to make him a bishop. He was a contemporary of Adomnan, and might well have come to see him in Glen Lyon. Perhaps the two saints exchanged handbells, as Columba and Kentigern had previously exchanged their pastoral staffs.

From the church where Cedd's bell hangs, a path goes north across the mountains and through the forest to the southern edge of Loch Rannoch. This is one way to Glen Lyon from the north, and people seeking Adomnan might have walked it. To reach Loch Rannoch from the northwest means crossing the boggy desolation of Rannoch Moor, in which there are no signs of any wandering saint, or of any who might have sought a hermitage in that bleak space, more isolated than any island. Barren and dangerous as it is, it could have formed part of the route from Loch Etive along Glen Etive to Glen Lyon, and as such it could have been crossed by St Blane's uncle, the learned Chattan, whose name is remembered in the ruins of Ardchattan Priory [49:972350] on the side of Loch Etive. These ruins are in the garden of a private house, but in the summer the public are allowed to walk to the remains of the thirteenth-century priory which Cromwell burned down in 1654. On the hillside above the gardens, and reached across the fields from the car park, are the remains of a church dedicated to a St Modan, but whether that dedication belongs to the sixth-century abbot of Stirling and Falkirk or to one of the eighth century, I have not been able to find out. The ruins lie by the route that anyone might take who was going southeast from Moluag's sanctuary of Lismore.

As for Adomnan, his way took him east to Fortingall, past the remains of the so-called Roman camp by the river. The ruins look like a circular cattle pound, except for their extraordinarily wide entrances and their walls which are about fourteen feet thick in some parts.

Adomnan died in his sanctuary in the glen in 704. His last wish was that his body should be carried along the length of the riverside on a bier, and that he should be buried at the place where the first thong (*dul* in Gaelic) that bound the corpse to the bier should break. That, at any rate, is how the traditional story goes, and it adds that the saint requested that a church and college were to be founded at the place of his burial.

Dull

By strange chance the bond broke at a place which was then called Tulli, and which has since been known by the name of Dull. This is a hillside village at the very end of Glen Lyon above the B846. At the east end of its church there is a mound, traditionally believed to be Adomnan's grave. Yet the history of Dull or Tulli goes back far beyond his time.

Burials that have been found here show that this place was inhabited from 3000 BC, and its reputation as a holy place of learning goes back to the first half of the first century, when Mensetus, a Pictish chief, returned to Rome with the ambassador who fathered Pontius Pilate. There he stayed long enough to hear St Peter preach, and this so inspired him that he became a convert to Christianity and brought the gospel back to his own people in the vale of Menzies.

We can probably discount this piece of clannish piety, which operates on about the same level as the Gaelic love of punning to explain the name of Dull. That story and the putative location of Adomnan's grave could not have failed to have enhanced the power and prestige of the sanctuary and monastery at Dull throughout the Middle Ages.

The hillside village, which was to become the site of the medieval monastery, was a Christian settlement of some stature by the mid-seventh century, and some accounts of the life of Adomnan describe his time in Glen Lyon as a period of twelve years which he spent as a recluse at Dull. However that may be, it was probably the existence and needs of the first Christian settlement at Dull that drew Adomnan east from Iona. About the same time it also attracted the young Cuthbert to journey north from the monastery at Melrose, as we shall see in the next chapter.

Dull's sanctuary was marked out by three crosses, two of which can be seen inside the old church at Weem a mile or two to the east. The third, one arm broken off by a runaway horse, stands at the road junction in the village. It served as a market cross until the village was deserted at the time of the clearances. A few new cottages have been built on the hillside, but nobody has made use of the patch of henbane-covered land behind the church where the Pictish-Christian college once stood.

Adomnan seems to have been known to the people east of Glen Lyon and to have lived for a while by the south banks of the Tay beyond Aberfeldy. Tomtayewen (the mound of Eonan's house) [52:885503] is the name of the site of a village which was deserted in the early nineteenth century. Some traces of the crofts remain, but there is nothing that proves any habitation in the seventh century. Yet it is likely that the saint was here, and in any case the place is worth visiting. The easiest way to find it is to look out for a roadside sign just to the west of Grandtully, which directs you to the ancient chapel of St Mary. A rough lane leads to that sixteenth-century church, hidden among farm buildings. Pause there before going on to Tomtayewen, for the ceiling of the chapel magnificently painted with fleshy angels and the family crests of the Earls of Athlone is not to be missed. The lost village is on the hillside to the south of the farm.

Fillan

There is a story that Fillan, nephew of Comgan, who founded a monastery at Loch Alsh, journeyed with Adomnan to Tyndrum. There they drew lots to see who should carry on to the east, and who should follow the river to the south. The latter allocation fell to Fillan, and that part of the River Dochart which runs between Tyndrum and Crianlarich still bears his name.

Loch Lomond

The trouble about the story is its dating, for Fillan belongs to the mid-eighth century. Born about the time of Adomnan's death, he came to Scotland with his widowed mother, who had resolved to end her days in the nunnery on the island of Inchcailloch in the southern waters of Loch Lomond. Ruins of a church can be seen on that island, whose name translated means 'the island of the old woman'; this has been taken to refer to Kentigerna, Fillan's mother.

The long, low island on which she ended her days stands out from the others in this part of the loch which are mainly heavily wooded, because of its lush meadows and its obvious signs of habitation. Every summer the waters around these islands are thronged with little boats as the loch's bonnie banks and braes fill up with city people snatching a few hours in this most accessible part of the Highlands. From the little marina of pleasure craft anchored at Balmaha a passenger-carrying mail boat makes a tour of the islands, and it provides the best chance of visiting Kentigerna's cell.

Her son established his monastery to the south of Tyndrum and just to the east of the river. The place where he settled is marked by the ruins of the medieval priory at 50:359284, where James IV stayed when he was on a hunting expedition in 1501. The ruins stand beside the old road running through the farmstead and agricultural research station of Kirkton, which has now become part of the West Highland Way. The priory, in this pleasant, fertile strath sheltered by the hills to the east, flourished until the twelfth century. Then it fell into a decline from which it was saved by Robert the Bruce, who gave it a royal endowment in gratitude for his victory at Bannockburn.

Bruce had reason to be grateful to St Fillan and to those who served his memory. Shortly after his coronation in 1306, he was forced to take refuge in the priory of Strath Fillan. While he was there he was visited by two of the Dewars (guardians of the saint's relics). One of them kept Fillan's pastoral staff or Quigrich (the word means a stranger, and the staff was so called because it was carried from place to place); the other his armbone, from which such a light gleamed when it was contained in his living body that the saint was enabled to write in the dark.

Fillan is supposed to have given these relics, together with three others, into the hands of five Dewars shortly before his death in 777. In return for their guardianship, each Dewar was given a croft and a small parcel of land. The Dewar of the Quigrich had his land in Strath Fillan, just across the river from the priory. Together with the Dewar of the armbone, he gave Bruce the Gaelic blessing of the old Columban Church, and both men, with their relics, accompanied the king to his successful encounter with the English at Bannockburn.

The other three relics of the saint were his handbell (now in the

National Museum of Antiquities in Edinburgh), whose Dewar's land was at Suie in Glen Dochart [51:482278], a place from which the saint often preached. The Dewar who took charge of Fillan's portable altar was given a croft near the chapel of Na Farig, whose ruins can still be seen near Auchlyne [51:512295]; and the Dewar of the Meser, which is taken to be the manuscript on which the saint was working at the time of his death, had lands at the head of Loch Tay at Killin.

Bruce was by no means the only person to benefit from the divine intervention of St Fillan, both in the saint's lifetime and long after his death. If you follow the West Highland Way through the farm buildings at Auchter Fyre to the north of the priory in Strath Fillan, you will find that the farm road takes you across a stream which cascades gently into the Dochart. Once across the bridge the way veers west to follow the course of the stream towards the river. Just beyond the place where the two waters meet, there is a pool which for centuries was believed to provide a cure for insanity. The treatment, which was practised well into the nineteenth century, was extremely tough.

The mad person was forcibly immersed in the pool, then taken back to the priory and tied to a wooden frame. His head was put into the stone font, still to be seen among the ruins, and then the saint's handbell (which by the seventeenth century was kept on the slab which was supposed to mark Fillan's grave) was placed above him. Covered in straw for warmth, the lunatic had to spend the night in this uncomfortable and eerie way. Next morning, the sign that a cure had taken place was found in a slackening of the ropes that bound the patient to the frame.

Killin

From the monastery that he founded, St Fillan's mission took him east along Glen Dochart, beneath the heights of Ben More, towards the head of Loch Tay at Killin. On the south bank of the glen, near the site of the present Suie Lodge Hotel, he settled one of the many preaching 'chairs' which he was to establish throughout west Perthshire.

Another such 'chair' was by the shallow Falls of Dochart at the western edge of the village of Killin. When he came here, it seems that a religion even older than Druidism was still flourishing. Perhaps the people were still held by the power of the two stone circles which stand at either end of Loch Tay. At Kenmore, on the eastern extremity of the loch, the Bronze Age circle of Croftmoraig [51:796474] stands in the woods where the waters of the Lyon and the Tay meet. This spot must also have marked the meeting place of the area in which the healthy 'ruddy-cheeked' Adomnan was honoured with the territory ministered to by Fillan, a man who, like Bruce himself, was rumoured to suffer from leprosy.

At Killin, the circle [51:577326] stands in the private grounds of Kinnell House. The quickest way to reach it is by the lane on the south side of the bridge which crosses the Falls of Dochart, by the entrance to the fortified island, which has been for centuries the burial ground of Clan MacNab. Possibly the men who built the first earth-works on that island were also responsible for placing the sacred stones in position. Sadly, since 1984 it is no longer possible just to walk up to the remaining stones of that circle (six still upright and one fallen) beside the walls of Kinnell House. Now you have to make an appointment before you can go through the gate at the end of the lane. You do that by arranging the visit through the tourist office in the village. This procedure is not a tribute to the antiquity of the stones. It has been introduced because the house has now been bought by the owner of Hercules, a wrestling bear, and it is the bear that people are making appointments to see.

To the west, across the river from the Kinnell circle, is a single standing stone [51:568328]. You will find it by going through the playing fields at the back of the school. It stands neglected in the middle of some swampy ground, although, as it was broken at some time, one half has been cemented on to the other. It is possible that the original worshippers at the circle looked west across the river to this stone, which at certain times of the year must have caught the last rays of the sun setting behind the hill of Meall Clachach. That would bear out the tradition that when Fillan came to Loch Tay he found the people worshipping the sun and the moon.

Over the years, however, a legend has grown claiming that the stone marks the grave of the warrior-hero Fingal. Could it be that over the centuries the fighting clansmen, who were still partly caught up in the old religion and resentful of the gospel of peace, tried to reclaim the stone for their own local cults? We shall find that much the same thing has happened with the stone that is said to mark Dermot's grave by Loch Nell.

To return to Fillan. When he reached the head of Loch Tay, he established his mill by a bridge, as Adomnan had done at Loch Lyon. A mill still stands at Killin in the place where Fillan first set one, powered by the waters of the Falls of Dochart. No millwheel turns now, but the building belongs to a firm of woollen merchants selling direct to the public, and anyone is free to enter it. If you do so you will be shown the stones which Fillan is said to have used to cure the sick. There are eight of them, three large and five small. Each one is thought to represent a different part of the body, and to have the power of healing its fleshly counterpart.

These therapeutic stones, which were used to treat ailments up to the nineteenth century, now rest on a sill on a bed of river wrack: straw and twigs from the Dochart. Every year on Christmas Eve the bedding is changed, and every year on St Fillan's Day (20 January) no work is done at the mill.

The most southerly point to be associated with Fillan (although some say it is related to a much earlier saint of the same name) is the village of St Fillans itself, at the eastern end of Loch Earn. Although none of the peaks rise to any great height, the mountainous region between Loch Earn and Loch Tay to the north is formidable. So we have to imagine that Fillan and his followers reached the southern loch by making their way through Glen Ogle on the same route as the A85 takes now. That road comes out at Lochearnhead at the western end of the loch. Fillan was to establish his 'chair' on a Pictish fort built on a 600-foot-high rocky outcrop that rises out of the birch-covered low ground at the eastern end of the loch.

The most level stretch of that ground has now been turned into a golf course. So to reach the rock of Dundurn [51/52:707234] you have to take the path which goes in front of the clubhouse and then turns left towards a farm road. The rock is now ahead of you across three meadows. A track takes you there, passing first an ancient circular burial ground and then a small, square sewage works. There is no track in the rather swampy field from which St Fillan's rock rises. The entrance to this 'dun' is carefully wired off to corral a herd of wild goats, with aristocratic swept-back horns, which clamber about its summit.

From its heights you look west to the birch woods along the southern shore of Loch Earn, and east towards the site of the old Roman fortification at Comrie. Nearer at hand is another stone circle [51:755225] hidden in the woods in a bend of the river. Perhaps it was the continued pagan practices of the people who lived around this river in the Dark Ages that brought Fillan here, in the same way that he had been drawn to Loch Tay.

Iona

Long after Adomnan and Fillan walked the western glens of Perthshire, people from all over Scotland were making their way to Iona. Some were going there as pilgrims to the place where Columba had worked and died; others, more ceremonially, were taking part in the funeral processions of kings who were being taken for burial on the holy island. This custom was to continue until the eleventh century, when the last royal body was brought to Iona. It belonged to Lulach, nicknamed the Foolish, a son of Lady Macbeth by her first marriage. He was laid to rest in the tomb by St Oran's Chapel beside his mother, stepfather and the murdered King Duncan.

From Dunadd and all parts of central Scotland, royal coffins were taken from Loch Feochan to Port nam Marbh [49:734278] on Mull, and from there overland to Fionnphort for Iona. The royal funeral parties embarked from the mainland by a rock that juts into the neck of Loch Feochan at 49:833225. It is called Carraig nam Marbh, the Rock of the Dead, because it was here that the coffins were laid until the tide was right and they could be carried abroad the black funeral galleys. The ships that sailed into Loch Feochan to collect that burden had to carry ballast of Ayrshire earth to steady them around the inlets of the west coast. It is that soil, they say, which accounts for the shallows at the entrance to Loch Feochan below Kilninver; while the chapel at which the funeral party sang their masses is thought to have been on the steep southern side of the loch's outlet to the sea. A church that stood here [49:823220] has now been deconsecrated and turned into a holiday house.

From the north and east, the funeral boats sailed to Mull, or perhaps directly to Iona, along the length of Loch Linnhe, taking up their sad burden at a little beach in a bay at North Ballachulish, variously known as St Bride's Bay or the Bay of the Footfall. There seems to be nothing special about this little pebbly beach now, separated from the sloping field behind it by a straggly hedge. A few small craft still use this natural landing place, which was once so notable.

This inconspicuous spot, which none of the crowds of holiday makers driving north over the bridge across the neck of Loch Leven could possibly notice, let alone stop at, has a long history. When the very road on which thousands, if not millions, of cars go north each summer was being widened, archaeologists took a last-minute look at the disturbed land. It was then that Professor Stuart Piggott discovered a tiny (1.5cm) wooden goddess, which he dated as belonging to the first century AD.

In the meadow above the beach, the rectangular site of a long-vanished building is marked by a low mound. Here, and here alone in this derelict parcel of land, the healing meadowsweet grows in profusion. Is it because it was a holy place, sanctified by the bodies of dead kings, that no crop has been grown here within living memory?

The living pilgrims went by other routes to Iona. Like most people today who make the initial stage of the journey by travelling north by train or car to Oban, the pilgrims of past ages walked in that direction from Loch Aweside. The route northwest across the mountains from the thirty-mile-long loch in its deep forest of conifers starts near Bernaline Lodge [55:971139], where a narrow lane goes through the trees and round the north bank of Loch Avich. At Lochavich House [55:937154] there is a turning to the north where a track runs along swampy ground at the edge of the forest, and leads on to the slopes of the mountains to the east of Loch na Sreinge. There is a bare landscape of high rocks and rivers. The path (as it has now become) follows one of them, the Allt Braglenmore, until it reaches Bragleenbeg House [49:910204].

At this point the better road goes west by the north shore of Loch Scammadale, but the bleak mountain path turns to the northeast, following the Allt a' Choromaig to Musdale [49:935221]. Here, a scree-spattered, partly surfaced road runs for five and a half miles through the mountains (where the new telephone lines are being set up). It comes out at the growing new village of Kilmore beside the main road to Oban. The old village [49:888249] consists of two or three cottages, a farm and the roofless walls of a church in which very free-ranging glossy chickens scratch around.

There was certainly no road here in 1773, when an intrepid Miss MacVicar, who was to become even better known as Mrs Grant of Laggan, wrote about her travels in *Letters from the Mountains*. It is easy to imagine her relief as she turned to follow the river to the west and looked towards the sea. 'My spirit exhilarated with the sight of

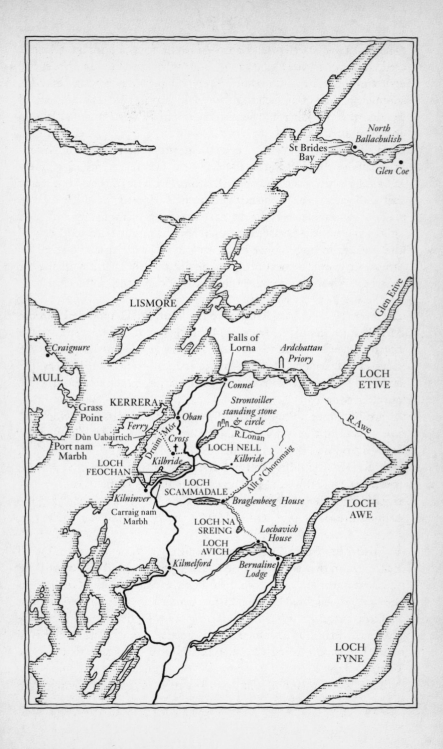

Glenfeochan,' she wrote. Later she went to a service in Kilmore church, which she described as an 'odd, old church'. When the service was over she went to the farmhouse, which in those days also served as an inn. She had done well to give thanks first for the safe outcome of her journey, for her route across the mountain wasteland was known to harbour robbers.

Walking that way now, even in daylight and with the distant company of the Telecom men on the far-off ridges, one can understand how uneasy she must have felt at times. The pilgrims, like many hill walkers, were in company. Part of their way would lie across marshy ground; even in the driest weather it is still squelchy on either side of this track. At least they would have been sure of water to add to the oatmeal which no doubt they carried with them. There are streams in the valley bottoms, and the silver birches which still line the crevices of the bar rock may indicate that in parts they walked through wooded glades.

Certainly Glen Feochan was much more thickly populated in the Middle Ages than it is now. At Kilbride [49:915245], by a farm to the north of the glen, there seem to have been a succession of at least three stone churches. The first was built in 802, the second in 1493, and the last in 1744, and that one was made large enough to hold three hundred people.

From Kilmore, the pilgrims did not go north to Oban, which did not exist until the coming of the railways. So instead, they took the western route to the other Kilbride [49:855258]. A cross (restored in recent years) stands by the track at 49:860258] as a reminder of their passing. From Kilbride a path goes over the hills to the coast. It meets the old drove road (still used for the cattle who are grazed on the penned meadows of Druim Mór) to the north of Dùn Uabairtich [49:834283].

Just to the west of that place the ferry still plies to the island of Kerrera, and that is the way the pilgrims went, making their crossing to Grass Point on Mull from the other side of the island. On Kerrera they would be joined by the pilgrims from the north, who would have had to take a boat across the Falls of Lora, which are now crossed by Connel Bridge. On the southern shore, they would make their way south by a route which is now marked out by the mountain road to Loch Nell.

This is a land of Neolithic chambered cairns and Bronze Age

barrows. At the eastern end of little Loch Nell, a circle of stumpy stones is just visible above the meadow grass below Strontoiller Farm [49:906294]. These stones are outmatched by the single standing stone by the roadside to the south of them [49:908289]. This stone is said to mark the place where the beautiful lad Diarmid died, tricked by the powerful Fingal, jealous of his wife's straying eyes. Fingal challenged Diarmid to a boar hunt, and so contrived his apparently accidental death. When the great creature was killed, Fingal insisted that the younger man should pace out the animal's length. In doing so a poisonous bristle entered his bare foot and he died instantly. The hill where this version of the mythological boar hunt is supposed to have taken place lies across the waters of the Lonan.

Whatever way one journeys across the country nowadays the ways to Iona for anybody without a boat of their own must start from Oban. If you have taken the pilgrims' walk from Loch Awe, then you can complete it by following the drove road from Dùn Uabairtich to the northeast over Druim Mór. From this green lane you will suddenly see the town as you approach the new housing estate by Pulpit Hill. Until 1770 Oban consisted of a single house, and it wasn't until thirty years later that it even became a village.

Throughout the Middle Ages, Kerrera was the natural place from which to embark for Iona. Many people must have thought of Columba as they set out from the mainland. One dramatic and tragic voyage is recorded. On 8 July 1249, Alexander II died on board his galley in Horseshoe Bay, on his way to try to regain control of the Hebrides. The tradition is that he made the crossing in defiance of a vision in which Columba himself had warned him against the undertaking.

✝

CHAPTER SEVEN

Cuthbert's Northumbria

By the roadside to the north of Hexham [87:936694] on the course of Hadrian's Wall above the North Tyne, a roughcast concrete cross marks the place where the Christian Oswald, who had been king of Northumbria for just a year, set up a wooden cross before the battle in which he defeated the pagan Cadwallern. The place became known as Heavenfield, and the year was 634. About that time Cuthbert was born, and for the next half-century his life was to be bound up with this war-torn region.

Even now it is impossible to visit Northumbria without being aware of the county's saint, a determined and kindly man of immense self-discipline and boundless goodwill. People speak of him with affection as Cuddy, which is the Border term for a donkey, a term also indeed used to describe the small, saddle-tank donkey engine – a 'fat cuddy' – which is commemorated in the bar of the Black Bull in Moffat. That the word is also used as an affectionate nickname for the saint must be attributed to his capacity for hard work, his modesty and his persistence. For although the austere Cuthbert had to be just as much a statesman as Columba, his negotiations were frequently carried out from a position of seclusion, and always with the minimum of fuss.

It is said that Oswald was encouraged before his victorious battle by a vision of Columba. Whether that was so or not, it is historically certain that one of his first acts afterwards was to send to Iona for a priest to minister to his people. Corman, the first monk to be sent, proved too stern and detached to make any headway with the Northumbrians, many of whom had lapsed into paganism. So he had to be replaced, and the next year, Aidan, an Irishman of noble birth, came to Oswald's palace at Bamburgh. A very much later and distantly imposing castle stands now on the promontory which was the capital of the region from 547, when the Anglian King Ida built his fortress on the site.

Lindisfarne

Aidan chose Lindisfarne, the long, thin island off the coast from Bamburgh, as the site for his church and monastic settlement. Although the island is accessible by causeway from the mainland at low tide, Aidan may well have had Iona in mind when he established himself there. Yet Lindisfarne was to be a base rather than a permanent home, for like the men of the Celtic Church before and after him, he spent most of his days travelling through the wild country and talking to anyone he encountered. In the early months he made these journeys in the company of Oswald, who had to act as his interpreter, for the only language that Aidan could speak was the Gaelic of Dalriada, a language which Oswald had learned as a child when he and his family were exiles on Iona.

When Aidan had learned enough of the tongue of the Angles of Northumbria, he chose to travel throughout the country on foot, steadfastly refusing the king's offer of a horse, because to ride would cut him off from the common people. He established schools as he went about on his missionary journeys, and worked for the freedom of those Celts who were held as slaves by the Anglian settlers.

Aidan's example of modest charity and care for the poor was followed by Oswald. At one Easter banquet, the king impulsively gave the silver vessel containing the main dish to the poor who crowded outside his hall. At that act, Aidan touched the king's right hand, saying 'May this hand never perish.' In 642, when Oswald was killed trying to quell a pagan uprising under Penda of Mercia at the Battle of Maserfelth (whose site has been equated with Oswestry), that arm was severed from his body. Throughout the Middle Ages it was kept in a silver reliquary in St Peter's Chapel in Bamburgh Castle, and became a focus of pilgrimage.

Ten years later, Aidan fell sick on one of his many journeys and was himself brought to Bamburgh. He stood at a place about a quarter of a mile to the north of the castle and, supported by his friends, looked across to Lindisfarne and died. One of the pillars in the present church, which bears Aidan's dedication, is supposed to mark the place where he died. At any rate Bamburgh church stands on the site where one of the first churches in Northumbria was built in Aidan's memory, two years after his death.

Cuthbert

On the day that Aidan died, Cuthbert, a lad of seventeen or so, was tending sheep on the Border hills, possibly on the southern slopes of the Lammermuirs, at a place that is marked now by the medieval fortification of Smailholm Tower [74:638348]. It stands on a piece of land flanked by the Leader Water to the west and the meandering Tweed to the south, where the vanished village of Wraxholm is sometimes given as Cuthbert's birthplace. Whether he was shepherding there, or on the Cheviots above the rich plain of Glendale, he must have known about the travelling bishop of Lindisfarne. So when he saw beautiful and unearthly lights in the sky taking on the shape of angelic forms, he was sure that he was watching Aidan's soul ascending to heaven. He took the vision as a sign that he was to follow that man's steps on earth.

We can only guess at Cuthbert's life before that decisive moment from a collection of legends about his birth and childhood, mostly of Irish origin, some of which are recorded in the life of the saint compiled by an anonymous monk of Lindisfarne. These stories suggest that although we know of him as a young shepherd, Cuthbert was of noble and probably of pagan birth. The legends tell us that he was the son of a Princess Sabina, and that his Christian destiny was foretold at the very moment he was being born. For at that time a bishop happened to pass the house, and saw that it was filled with such a burning light that it appeared to be wrapped in flame, although, like Moses's burning bush, it remained unconsumed.

The baby grew into a lively, spirited boy who loved to play and sport with other children and who never grew tired of running and jumping about. One day, while he was having fun with his friends, a petulant and precocious three-year-old child started to abuse him. 'Be steadfast and leave this foolish play,' he cried, and he wept when his words were disregarded. Then, addressing the young Cuthbert as 'Holy Bishop', he went on to rebuke him for 'these unnatural tricks done to show off your agility' which were not fitting for his high office. Small wonder that Cuthbert should recall such an incident in later life.

The legends agree that, from the age of eight, Cuthbert was brought up in a Christian household by his foster mother, Kenswith. This could mean that his parents had died, or more probably that they were following the tradition of other noble families of that time in sending their son away from home to learn manly skills, much as boy children in England were once sent to boarding schools. Wherever it was, Kenswith's household seems to have been more kindly than such institutions, and it was while he was living there that Cuthbert had his vision. His response was to leave the sheep in the care of his foster family, and to walk a few miles westward to the monastery that then stood above a bend in the River Tweed, a little to the east of the present Melrose.

Melrose

That name is derived from *mull ross*, which means a bare promontory, and indeed the place that was to become Cuthbert's home for many years still seems so in cold or wild weather. On the east side of the river sheer grey and red cliffs drop down to the water; on the west a smooth, green haugh ending in a shingle beach juts into the Tweed. Above that pasture the woods rise steeply, and on those heights the monastery stood. One of the monks was Eata, who was later to become Cuthbert's close friend and companion, and it was ruled over by the wise Boisil, an Irishman, who immediately accepted the shepherd lad into his novitiate.

There is nothing left of that monastery now. The site below it looks its best and most romantic from a viewpoint to the east of the river [74:593343], much beloved of Sir Walter Scott. He often stopped to gaze at it from the road that runs below Bemersyde Hill; and it was here, due to an 'accident' worthy of one of the stories of the saints, that the novelist's funeral procession was halted inadvertently.

If you decide to go down to the haugh, taking the green lane [74:579339] from the A68 which separates the estate of Old Melrose from the town, you may find fly-fishermen standing in the river, with their cars parked in the woodland. Above the primrose banks that separate the haugh from the trees, there are a few scant signs of the seventh-century abbey. Its stones lie embedded and covered with moss in the path through the woods above the walled garden at Old Melrose; one cheerful engraved face grins out from among the bricks of the back wall of the house; and to the north of the lane, a block incised with Celtic designs forms the lintel of the Edwardian summer-house by the swamp – all that remains of the monks' fish ponds. The intricate, angular designs on that stone were matched for me by the

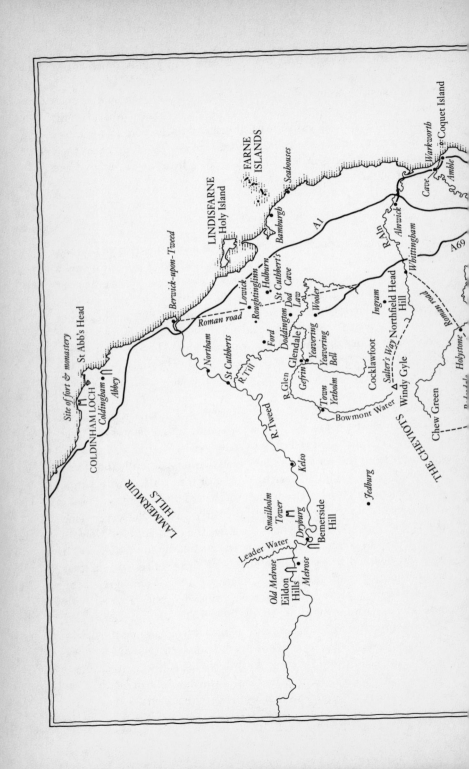

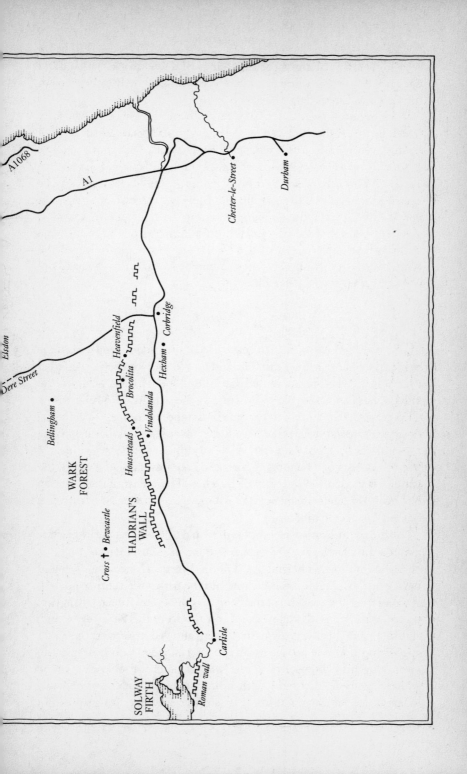

seemingly artificial and stilted markings of a woodcock, which I saw out on the open on a nearby path, away from the shady undergrowth for which its camouflage is designed.

Five hundred years after Cuthbert's death, the abbey of Melrose, which he knew, was replaced by the one whose substantial ruins stand by the river in Melrose town beneath Eildon Hill. That abbey was one of four set up during the reign of David I in the first half of the twelfth century. The others are at Kelso, Jedburgh and Dryburgh on the opposite bank of the Tweed from Old Melrose. Here Sir Walter Scott and Field Marshal Douglas Haig lie among the trees and the stones of a ruined abbey, which has more lively reminders of the past in the shape of the shelf marks of the bookstore in the cloister, and the scratched design for the Norman game of Merilies, or Nine Men's Morris, on a piece of pavement.

Weem

While he was at Melrose, Cuthbert started out on his wanderings. He made a January sea voyage to Fife, and on a longer journey travelled to the Picts on Tayside. At some time before 660 he went north to the village that is now known as Weem, a name which could refer to the cliffs above it which were to become his temporary home. To get there now you must go through Aberfeldy, crossing the Tay by one of the most magnificent of General Wade's bridges. Today the village of Weem consists of a handful of cottages, two inns (at one of which the general stayed in 1753) and two churches. The oldest of these, which has been the mausoleum for the Menzies clan since 1839, carries a St Cuthbert dedication.

Although the saint is supposed to have made his headquarters about a mile farther to the west at Adomnan's settlement of Dull, he chose Weem for his hermitage. The cave in which he is supposed to have made his shelter is unsafe now, but the path which climbs up to it, starting from the east end of the village by the Hotel Aileen Chraggan, was waymarked with yellow bands on the trees in 1983. Yet in high summer thick undergrowth had been allowed to cover the path, suggesting that few people make the pilgrimage now. Those who do eventually find themselves at the well, a patch of swampy ground which never goes dry in the hottest summer and which is formed on a ledge above the cave. Cuthbert is said to have called this water out from the bare rock so that he could follow his rigorous practice of immersing himself in cold water as he recited the Psalms.

Beside this place, he, or some other holy hermit, erected a tall cross. The stone stood for hundreds of years until it was broken by twentieth-century vandals and flung over the cliff face. Hamish MacDonald, keeper of both the cave and the old kirk, rescued the fragments and housed them in the church beside the Menzies' graves.

Weem has never been a very fortunate place. In Cuthbert's time the 'king' of the area, angered perhaps by the saint's popularity, accused him of seducing his daughter. Cuthbert, who showed that he could be as firm in his wrath as Columba, prayed to God, and immediately the ground at the feet of the wretched girl opened and swallowed her up. I like to think that if that happened she really only fell into the underground passage, guarded by five iron gates, which the old ballad tells us stretched from the cave of Weem to Loch Glassie a few miles to the north.

Eventually Cuthbert and Eata were sent south from Melrose to the monastery at Ripon, where for some years the younger man served as guest-master. In that capacity he had another angelic vision. A beautiful but travel-worn wayfarer rode up to the monastery. Cuthbert's first duty was to provide the visitor with water to wash. He did so, and then, leaving him, went to prepare his food. When he returned with the meal, the visitor had disappeared; the only sign that anyone had been in the room where he was washing were three white loaves made of the finest flour.

While he was at Ripon, Cuthbert first became aware of the troubles caused by the clash between Roman and Celtic Christian practices, which had been somewhat arbitrarily resolved at the Synod of Whitby in 663. Brought up and trained by monks who were schooled in the Irish tradition of Iona, he was an adherent of the old ways. This meant that both he and Eata, who appears to have felt the same way, were found to be too much of a disturbing influence in a place dominated by the urbane Wilfrid, a staunch supporter of Rome. So once more Cuthbert found himself at Melrose. There he became the close companion of Boisil, now well advanced in years, and soon to die of the so-called yellow plague, which spread north from Kent and Essex, reaching Melrose and Lindisfarne in 664.

Just before Boisil died, Cuthbert was struck down with the sickness, and throughout one night his life hung in the balance. The monks all prayed that he might be spared to them, and his response was characteristic. As soon as he felt the slightest sign of returning energy, he called for his staff and sandals and got up from his bed to go about his duties. The chief of these was to attend to his old teacher in his last illness, reading a section of St John's Gospel with him every day.

Lindisfarne

When Boisil died, Cuthbert became prior of Melrose, but he was soon moved from there to Lindisfarne, for when Eata was appointed as abbot of the island monastery founded by Aidan, Cuthbert, then aged about thirty, became its prior. He was chosen for his good sense and discretion in managing a community in constant danger of being bitterly divided by the conflicts between the Roman and the Celtic Churches. Lindisfarne had never been staunchly in favour of the Church of Rome; for Finan, who succeeded Aidan as abbot, and who resembled him closely in character, had always firmly defended the Irish customs against the changes that were being introduced from abroad. However, he was wide enough in his sympathies to allow the ambitious Wilfrid, who was then one of his monks, to journey to the Holy City.

It was Finan who built the wooden church of Lindisfarne which Cuthbert must have found when he came to the island, which was not known as Holy Island until the eleventh century. Cuthbert came to take up his duties at low tide, walking along the pilgrims' way from Beal Sands. This route is still marked by guideposts, and it crosses the stretch between Lindisfarne and the mainland a little to the south of the present motor road, which has made access so easy now that several of the native-born islanders complained to me that the character of their homeland has been miserably abused and completely changed. Yet Cuthbert would still be at home among the multitude of birds, rejoicing in his own precious eider ducks and the plump, gliding fulmars. And apart from the cross put up to mark the spot where he built his special chapel, nothing has altered the grass-covered basalt rock of Hobthrush which is joined to the southwest corner of the island at low tide.

Motorized pilgrims come here now, drawn by the stories of Cuthbert, to watch the birds and to look at the ruins of the medieval

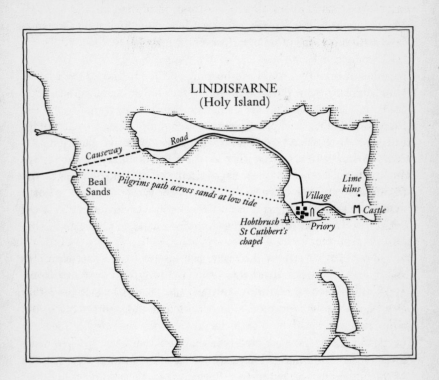

priory. They flock to the sixteenth-century castle on the rock at the southeastern edge of the island, entering it beneath a portcullis that is part of Edward Lutyens' fanciful restoration of the building in 1903. Many delight in the formal walled garden which his friend Gertrude Jekyll laid out in the middle of the surrounding fields.

Beyond the castle are the vast nineteenth-century limekilns, a permanent reminder that lime-burning rivalled fishing as the island's main industry from the Middle Ages. The limekilns have long been cold and ruined, but there is a small crab-fishing fleet moored in the island's harbour, on whose shores the tarred, upturned hulks of older boats make stores and workshops. Lindisfarne's main industry now is tourism; but despite the day visitors, the mead distillery, the gift shops and the fact that most of the village is made up of holiday cottages, the farmland stretching down to the east and the sand dunes to the north make this a place of charm and peace. Because of anxieties about the tides, few day visitors venture far away from village, priory and castle rock.

Like Aidan, Cuthbert took Lindisfarne as a base from which to travel, and it is perhaps from this period of his life that the stories grew up about his particular affinity with animals. He was especially protective of the brown-speckled eider ducks and their smart black and white mates, all puffed up with the down which they use to line their nests; but it is with other creatures that he is supposed to have had a miraculous communion. There are stories of the ways that animals fed him while he was on his travels. Perhaps it was just coincidental that an eagle should happen to drop a salmon into the boat in which the ravenous saint and his companions were rowing down the Tyne; but no natural explanation will do for the horse who pulled away the thatch from the roof of a hut to reveal meat and bread wrapped up in a fine cloth and ready for Cuthbert's dinner.

Coldingham

The most pleasing story about Cuthbert and the animals arose from a visit that he made to the abbey of Coldingham, on the height of St Abb's Head to the north of Berwick. While he was there a monk saw him leave his dormitory at night, and watched as the saint descended the steep cliffs to the sea and entered the water, where he stood until morning reciting the Psalms. At dawn, when the frozen Cuthbert scrambled out to the rocks of the shore, two little sea creatures (Bede calls them otters) came and dried his feet with their fur. This story of the saint's affinity with animals has a bitter twist for anyone who visits Coldingham now and goes down to the tiny harbour to the south of St Abb's Head, when the crab-fishing boats are being met by the transport lorries, and the living creatures are shoved into overflowing crates for their final journey.

The whole of the headland now belongs to the Scottish National Trust, and is rich in interest for geologists, naturalists and archaeologists. It is especially marked by the contrast between the wild sea cliffs to the east, and the rich farmland to the west. Cuthbert must have found this too, for the place he came to was a rich foundation. Within a few years of his visit, St Ebbe's Abbey was to become notorious for its luxurious living, which is perhaps why the saint felt compelled to exercise his own ascetic disciplines with redoubled vigour.

Ebbe

Ebbe, the first abbess of Urbs Coludi, which she founded, was some twenty years older than Cuthbert. The daughter of Edwin's predecessor as king of Northumbria, half-sister of Oswald and aunt of Etheldreda, founder of the cathedral at Ely, she was a woman of great power and influence. Yet she had reason to be troubled. Having spent her childhood on Iona she felt a loyalty to the Celtic Church, yet in matters of administration she was a supporter of Wilfrid and the practices of Rome. It was natural that she should want to talk this over with Cuthbert, who had himself been taught at Melrose by the Irish Boisil.

The site of the monastery at which they met does not coincide with the ruins of the medieval priory which you will find in the village of Coldingham. Ebbe had her double monastery to the north of that on the heights between St Abb's Head and Coldingham Loch, possibly where an Iron Age fort once stood [67:898687].

Elfled

In 684, Cuthbert travelled south. He was going to have a similar conversation with Oswy's daughter, Elfled, who came north from her abbey of Whitby. The two met on Coquet Island, a couple of miles out at sea from the mouth of the river which is now edged with the seaside town of Amble. Elfled, who had succeeded the wise and powerful Hilda as abbess of Whitby on the latter's death in 680, also inherited from her the worries about the rival forms of church government. Perhaps she took Cuthbert for her soul friend. At any rate, she certainly seems to have followed his calm, common-sense methods in dealing with ideological disputes. We are told that at one time she was cured of paralysis by touching his girdle, and that story could relate to a form of psychological disturbances the disputes drove her to.

The only important building on the fourteen-acre Coquet Island now is its lighthouse, but in the eighteenth century the ruins of a monastic cell were reported on its western coast. Perhaps that is where Cuthbert and Elfled met, and perhaps they were joined in their deliberations by the solitary who lived in the spacious cave [81:245059] across the river from Warkworth Castle, which has a fifteenth-century chapel incorporated in it, but which certainly must have been a dwelling long before that. It is just the sort of place that a Celtic monk would choose for a retreat, but that is speculation. Still, Cuthbert would surely have known of the church dedicated to Aidan and Oswald in Warkworth town, and which changed its allegiance to St Lawrence when his relics were sent over from Rome, perhaps to soften the Celtic adherents at the Synod of Whitby.

The visits that Cuthbert made to Ebbe and Elfled were unusual; most of his travels took place nearer home among the people of his native hills. These are wild and wide enough to provide many days' journeying, and often he had to stay away from Lindisfarne for several nights, and would even sleep in a tent after he became bishop rather than leave any settlement unvisited.

We can follow some of the routes he must have taken over the hills which flank the wide fertile valley of Glendale, which was to be one of the main areas of agricultural reforms in the eighteenth century. Signs of its enclosure can still be read here, for in a county of stone walls, the vale is parcelled up in quickset hedges.

For Cuthbert the hills nearest to home were those that run north-west from Dod Law [75:006317] to the north of the River Till. A solitary shepherd's house stands on these heights now, and today it can make the centre of a good circular walk of four or five miles. You start the climb from the footpath that leaves the road from Doddington signposted to Wooler golf course. As you climb through the steep bracken slopes of the western side of the hill, you can look across the valley of Glendale to the Cheviot Hills which retain their snow late into the spring.

Approached from this side, the shepherd's house seems virtually inaccessible, and yet there are net curtains in the windows and lovingly arranged china on the ledges. Habitation starts to the north of the house, where the golf course starts on the farther side of two large hill forts, both once protected by double earthworks. Several rings of stones mark the dwellings of the people who lived in the one to the west, and which still may have served as shepherds' shelters when Cuthbert walked here.

From the triangulation point that now stands in the one to the east, the path goes downhill through the heather towards pastures out of which another hill fort rises [75:013328]. Here the massive slabs which mark the western entrance are adorned with cup and ring marks. On a spring morning the skylarks, curlews and hares are the busy ones here. Apart from one or two enthusiastic golfers and the occasional farmer, you will meet nobody on this hill, where Cuthbert might have talked with many families, and which was certainly heavily populated in Iron Age and Roman times.

The circular walk goes southwest past the golf course to Doddington, but if you turn right along the lane from the fort, cross the Roman road that runs south from Lowick, follow the lane south-east to the Coal Burn and then turn north to Holborn Grange [75:050350], you will come to some National Trust land and directions for finding St Cuthbert's Cave.

St Cuthbert's Cave

This cave is a natural rock shelter in the new pine woods. For thousands of years it must have been the home of people who collected their food from the moors and the shore, and up to the nineteenth century it was used as a shelter by shepherds. It has long been associated with Cuthbert. Some say it was here that he slept when, as prior and then as bishop of Lindisfarne, he went travelling among his people; others have it that his uncorrupted body lay here when, a hundred years or more after his death, his followers took their most precious relic out of the clutches of the Danes.

The walk up to the cave from Holburn Grange starts by climbing up a green lane, flanked in spring on one side by banks of white violets.

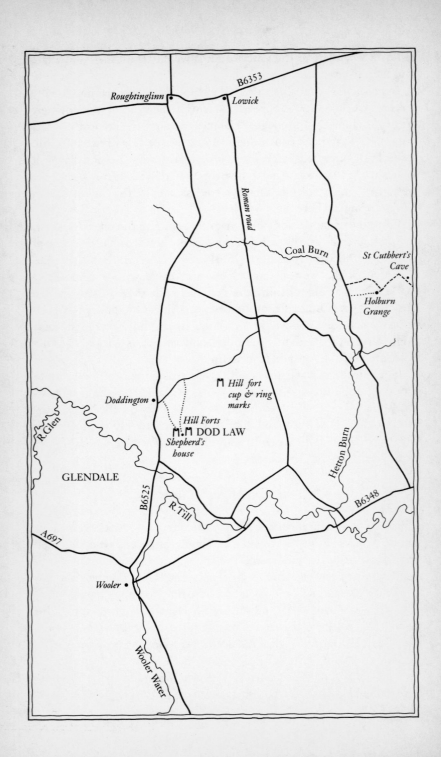

B6353

Roughtinglinn • • Lowick

Roman road

Coal Burn

St Cuthbert's Cave

Holburn Grange

ⵎ *Hill fort cup & ring marks*

Doddington •

Hill Forts
ⵎ⋮ⵎ DOD LAW
Shepherd's house

R.Glen

GLENDALE

B6525

R.Till

Hetton Burn

B6348

A697

Wooler •

Wooler Water

When you get to the woods, you will find that somebody has planted daffodils in the clearing that leads to the cave. They will be better when they have run wild and scattered like the wood sorrel that carpets the ground between the trees. The place is partly a memorial to a First World War widow, Mildred Louise Leather, who died in 1966 at the age of ninety-one, and whose name is inscribed on the high weather-worn boulder at the cave's entrance. Less officially, people have been writing their names here, sometimes with attempts at decorative skill, since the early nineteenth century. It takes about a hundred years for such vandalism to become acceptable.

More treasured and certainly much more mysterious rock inscriptions can be seen a few miles to the west at Roughringlinn [75:977370], a prehistoric settlement standing at the head of a gorge between Lowick and Ford. Here at the northwest edge of the Doddington Ridge is a rocky outcrop inscribed with intricate mazelike spirals and carefully rounded cup marks. These are said to be the finest in an area noted for such inscriptions, but although we may be able to compare them, no one has yet read their true meaning.

Yeavering

Across Glendale, going west from the chief Cheviot town of Wooler, the kings of Northumbria had their palace at Yeavering, near the plain where there are signs of Neolithic burials and rituals and below the intricate hill fort on Yeavering Bell. Now all that is left of the palace is a plaque by the B6351 [74:925304] telling passers-by that the place was once known as Gefyn, and that it was from here that Paulinus baptized his converts in the River Glen about five years before Cuthbert was born. Paulinus is supposed to have spent over a month at Yeavering or Gefyn. Because of its Christian importance, Yeavering palace was destroyed by the pagan Cadwaller after Edwin of Northumbria was defeated and killed in 633. It is not too fanciful to imagine that Cuthbert would have found it a suitable place for pilgrimage.

There are no roads across the Cheviots today. The few lanes that wind down the valleys all end at the last farmhouse. In Cuthbert's time people seem to have been hardier, and we can imagine that he would have been familiar with the packhorse teams that used the Salter's Way and the Roman road of Dere Street. The Salter's Way starts at

Northfieldhead Hill [81:984122] about four miles to the south of Ingram, where you can now find the Cheviot Information Centre, and which could well have had a church in Cuthbert's lifetime, for we know that there was one standing there which had to be restored in 1060. The path across the hills crosses the border into Scotland, where it coincides with the Pennine Way to the north of Windy Gyle, and makes for Cocklawfoot [80:853186] and the lane which follows Bowmont Water to Town Yetholm.

Dere Street, which runs as the A68 from Corbridge south of the Roman wall, and crosses the hills from Redesdale Camp [80:827988] to the remains of other Roman camps at Chew Green [80:788085] by Coquet Head, runs into the army danger zone at its northern end and is not always accessible to walkers.

Another Roman road came southwest from Whittingham on the River Aln and ran west to Dere Street. It crossed the River Coquet just above Holystone [81:955027], a village that gets its sanctity more from its well than from any stone. This well is in fact a little Roman reservoir, which still supplies the village with its water. One tradition has it that it was here rather than at Yeavering that Paulinus baptized his flocks of converts, and another that the well was blessed more than two centuries before by Ninian. A medieval statue of one or other of those saints, brought to the place from Alnwick in the nineteenth century, now graces the waterside, which gets it name of Lady's Well from the Augustinian canonesses who dedicated it to the Virgin.

Once again it is reasonable to suppose that Cuthbert might have made his own pilgrimage here, and I like to think that it was somewhere among these hills that he made his decision to retire from his busy wandering life and seek permission to spend the rest of his years as a solitary on a small island. He was then about forty years old.

CHAPTER EIGHT

From Inner Farne to Durham Cathedral

From Lindisfarne you can look south across seven miles of sea to the island of Inner Farne and the other bird-covered basalt rocks that rise above the surface of the waves to the east of it. Cuthbert knew that Aidan had often made short retreats to the Farne Islands, so in 675, when he felt overpressed by much travelling and lack of privacy (Bede tells us that he had to share the common dormitory on Lindisfarne), he sought and received permission to resign his work as prior and spend the rest of his days as an island solitary.

The Farne Islands are divided from the mainland by rough and treacherous seas, but they are fairly close inshore, and from his retreat Cuthbert could see the fortress of Bamburgh Castle in almost any weather. Today the inheritors of his isolation are the three men on Longstone lighthouse, who are relieved by helicopter every twenty-eight days, the RSPB's summer wardens, who live in the cottage on Brownsman Island that was Grace Darling's home when her father was lighthouse keeper, the crowding birds they observe and protect, and a large colony of grey seals.

Grace Darling

It is just possible, though rather unlikely, that when Cuthbert came to Inner Farne, a few of the pigmy descendants of the people who lived on the mainland in the Bronze Age still scraped a meagre living on the outer islands. If so, they could be the source of the tradition that Cuthbert had to banish evil spirits to the outer Farnes. From there they are supposed to have raised the storms which lured the tormented souls of shipwrecked sailors to the place and brought others to their deaths. The toll of wrecks on the Farnes is horrifically long, but the one generally remembered is that of the ill-fated *Forfarshire* which founded on 7 September 1838. Her memory

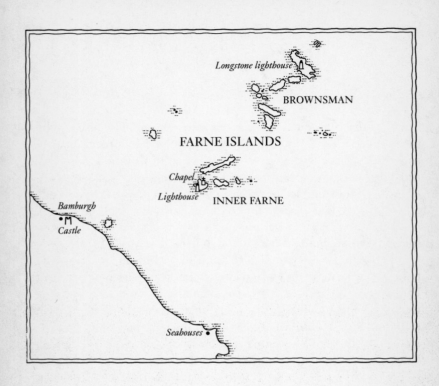

Longstone lighthouse

BROWNSMAN

FARNE ISLANDS

Chapel

Lighthouse

INNER FARNE

Bamburgh

Castle

Seahouses

remains green because of the much acclaimed courage of Grace Darling, the nineteen-year-old girl who helped her father rescue nine survivors from the rocks. Her death from tuberculosis seven years later provided a perfect theme for Victorian sentimentalism. The cottage in Bamburgh village where she died is marked by a plaque, and opposite the churchyard, where her body lies in canopied splendour, there is a museum – some have called it a shrine – displaying any object that has the remotest connection with her short life or that of the *Forfarshire* disaster.

Inner Farne

On Inner Farne, the most spacious of the islands, Cuthbert built a circular beehive hut of earth and stone, in the old style. While he was building it, a crow somehow managed to destroy the work he was doing on the roof. When Cuthbert rebuked the bird, it flew away but returned three days later to ask pardon for the wanton act, and to bring a lump of grease for the saint's shoes. In any case, Cuthbert intended to leave a small opening in his roof so that he could have some light and see the sky, for he denied himself any windows which would distract his attention from his contemplation of God. Beside his hut he built a small rectangular oratory and a guest house for his visitors. The place on which they stood is now taken up by a chapel, built in 1400.

Now summer visitors make regular boat trips to the islands from the seaside town of Seahouses. They come to look at the nesting birds on the ledges of the cliffs and watch the seals at the farthest point to the east. The two inner islands belong to the National Trust, and on both these the birds are protected by the RSPB which means that nobody can land there during the nesting season. So the best time to take one of the tourist boat trips to the islands is in April and early May. Then you can spend a couple of hours being taken by the boatmen under the pinnacles whose heights are lined with the penguin-like guillemots, and where each rock shelf is inhabited either by the smooth, white, tender-looking kittiwakes, or by pairs of the more dramatic tufted shags, their black plumage glistening with green sheen. Farther out on the rocks by the lighthouse, the grey seals rear out of the water, watching the progress of the boat with an alert intelligence, while the chief bull rests unperturbed on an exposed rock.

One of the boatmen doubles as postman to the lighthouse, and on a good day you can land there and be taken up into the lamp chamber by one of the Trinity House men on his tour of duty. From the tower you look west across the islands to the mainland and the snowcapped Cheviots on the skyline; to the northwest is the mass of Bamburgh Castle which is at its most impressive seen from the sea.

On its return voyage the boat passes the place where Grace Darling and her father undertook the rescue of the men clinging to the storm-dashed rocks, and then it bears south to slide up to the beach which forms the little harbour of Inner Farne. This is the place where all the people who came on pilgrimage to see Cuthbert must have landed. A medieval tower stands over the place where he lived alone in his beehive cell. Next to it is the chapel, and in the centre of this complex of buildings, which includes a shed housing the National Trust's display of the island's wildlife, is the holy well from which Cuthbert drew his water supply. On this flat part of island he grew his scant crop of barley.

At the southwestern end of the island, by the low, white buildings of the automatic lighthouse, the cliffs house thousands of jostling seabirds. Shags, guillemots and kittiwakes struggle for nesting space on every rock ledge, while puffins prospect among the burrows on the grassy slopes for the underground home that will house their single offspring. From the north coasts of Inner Farne you look across the stretch of water that lies between this frequently storm-bound island and the easily accessible Lindisfarne. Could it be that Cuthbert chose this remote home for another reason besides the natural desire of the religious to be where nothing will distract his attention from God? A wise and kindly man, he must have been well aware that many people would come to seek his help and advice, indeed his guest house proves that he encouraged them to do so; but he was also perceptive enough to appreciate that his help would be more valued if people had to risk a difficult and sometimes dangerous sea voyage to obtain it.

During the ten years that Cuthbert spent on Inner Farne, he kept closely in touch with church affairs, and was so well regarded for his patient good sense that, as disputes on church government grew more bitter, he was asked to arbitrate with the authority that a bishopric would confer on him. He was most reluctant to take on that position. Bede gives an account of the many messengers who went in vain to the island imploring Cuthbert to return as a bishop to the mainland.

Finally Trumwine, bishop of the Picts, with a host of other religious and powerful men, took boat for Farne. When Cuthbert met them 'they all knelt down and adjured him in the name of the Lord, with tears and prayers, until at last they drew him, also shedding many tears, from his sweet retirement and led him to the synod. When he had come, in spite of his reluctance he was overcome by the unanimous will of them all and compelled to submit his neck to the yoke of the bishopric.' His submission was somewhat tempered. Although he agreed to be consecrated as a bishop, he managed to exchange the diocese of Hexham to which he was called for that of Lindisfarne, which he found more acceptable. So he returned to his own priory and, one hopes, although Bede does not say so, that he then had a room of his own.

Hadrian's Wall

Whether he did or not, it was not long before he was on the road again, making visits to isolated settlements in his diocese. He made at least two journeys to Carlisle, presumably taking the route marked out by the ruins of the Roman wall, which were probably still quite substantial then. An overhanging rock to the west of the fort (now a museum) at Housesteads [87:789687] is known as Cuddy's crag; and Cuthbert could perhaps have made a detour from there, going north across the moor on the route through Wark Forest now taken by the Pennine Way, and so come to the present village of Bellingham. The stone-roofed twelfth-century parish church there carries his dedication, and between the churchyard and the river a lane leads down to Cuddy's Well [80:834834]. It takes the form of an octagonal stone marking a continual flow of water.

A little to the east of Cuddy's Crag on the wall is the stone outline of a mile fort, which was guarded in Roman times by fifty Belgian or German legionaries. It is hard to imagine how this country would have appeared to Cuthbert. Walking along this stretch of the wall in a bleak April with intermittent, stinging showers of hail, I wondered how he would have greeted the ominous grey-headed crows. To the north of the wall, beneath the steep crags, black cattle moved purposefully across the country to drink from the field drains. That, I thought, would possibly have caused him to think a little about new methods of farming, which have made good pasture of marshy ground, yet it would not seem too unfamiliar, and he would probably have recognized the circular stone cattle pounds which are still in use on these hillsides. His main astonishment would have been reserved for the orderly lines of conifers which make up the new forest.

It is impossible to know how much of the wall and the Roman buildings remained when he walked here, or whether he and his followers viewed these buildings of a past civilization with the same dread that we find in the Anglo-Saxon poem *The Ruin*, which was composed at about the same time and which refers to the city of Bath. Here in the north, Cuthbert and his followers on their way to Carlisle must have seen the grassy mounds among the falling walls of the Roman fort at Housesteads, and the remains of the more substantial township of Vindolanda on the Roman road of Stanegate a mile or so to the south. This has now been carefully excavated and interpreted. All is Roman now, and nothing is left to show that this was a main highway right through the Dark Ages.

As he travelled on to Carlisle from Hexham along Stanegate, Cuthbert must have been aware of the Mithraic temple a few miles to the north below the camp of Brocolita [87:862710]. This fort, which is still unexcavated, was inhabited from 134 to 383. Its grassy earthworks stand by the vallum of the wall, and on the summit of its flat enclosure worked slabs of stone lie among the sheep runs and nettles. When Cuthbert came here, the ruined buildings, whose stones were to provide walls for new fields centuries later, may still have been standing. Did he shudder as he peered into the ruins of the pagan place of worship? The narrow temple of Mithras, which served the officers of the fort, lies in the valley to the south of it. Its timbers were preserved in this boggy ground until the twentieth century. Situated among the bare hills where curlews call and dogs respond to the shepherd's whistle, it is still a powerful place to visit, even though the altar stones and the statues of the goddess at the entrance are replicas. Cuthbert may have seen the real things.

One account of his journey to Carlisle tells us that he was taken to see the Roman walls in that city, but there are now records of his comments. It is easier to speculate about his meetings there with his old friend Hereberht, who lived as a recluse on an island in Derwent Water by the town of Keswick. They were both to die at the same moment on the same day (20 March) in 687, as Cuthbert had prophesied they would. It was the year following their last meeting.

Cuthbert had held the office of bishop for only a couple of years when he felt that his end was near. So he resigned his see and retired again to Inner Farne to spend his last days in seclusion. He was only just over fifty, and it is thought that the austerity he had subjected himself to had accentuated the damage which his body had suffered from the plague which he had contracted as a young man at Melrose. There is also a theory evolved from observations made of his exhumed skeleton that he suffered from tuberculosis. Perhaps both causes contributed to his comparatively early death.

The death of Cuthbert

Bede tells the story of Cuthbert's end, and he took it from Abbot Herefrith, who was with the saint in his last hours – but not until his last hours. For although the monks came regularly from Lindisfarne to Inner Farne to visit their sick friend and teacher, who had demanded to be left alone on the island at night, a storm of such intensity blew up during the last week of his life that no boat could put out on the waters for five days. With only five raw onions to supply him with nourishment and moisten his lips, the dying saint confronted all the demons of hell. Apparently deserted by every other creature, he endured a torment of doubt and fear, confessing to Herefrith, when the abbot was at last able to make the crossing, that 'My adversaries have never persecuted me so frequently during all the time I have been living on this island as during these five days.'

Herefrith and his companions had found their old friend desperately ill and weak, sitting in the guest house that he had built for his visitors, and making the excuse that he did not want to give them the trouble of entering his cell. Herefrith's first task was to bathe the saint's swollen and ulcerated foot and to nourish him with a little warm wine. When Cuthbert had been thus restored, he asked to return to his own cell, and there, a few hours later, he died at peace among his friends. His body was taken back to the church at Lindisfarne for burial, but not for everlasting rest.

Even death could not put an end to the travels of Cuthbert's body. Bede tells us that among his last words to his companions was the command that his bones should be lifted from the tomb and carried 'to rest wherever God may decree' before the monks of Lindisfarne should be forced in any way to 'consent to iniquity'. So when the

Danes invaded the island in 793, his will was done and seven men bore off Lindisfarne's most precious relics: the uncorrupted body of Cuthbert, the gospels which had been transcribed in his honour (one of which was long believed to be that Gospel of John which he read to the dying Boisil at Melrose), and Oswald's skull. For seven years they took this burden around the diocese, and when that became unsafe they went farther afield. It was a long and often a terrifying journey; and it was to be a couple of centuries before the coffin, engraved with angels and archangels, the apostles and the Virgin and Child, was to reach its final resting place.

Monks carrying Cuthbert's body went as far west as Galloway, and their flight is still commemorated in the name of Cuthbert's town of Kirkcudbright. Some say that the bearers reached Whithorn, from where they intended to go to Ireland. The severity of the weather made that sea crossing impossible, so they turned south and east to Chester-le-Street, which they reached in 833, nearly forty years after they had retreated from Lindisfarne. It was Bishop Eardulph who brought Cuthbert's body to the place where, as a youth, the saint had been fed by the food which his horse found under the thatch of a shieling.

Right across the north country there are places in which Cuthbert's body is reported to have lain during the flight from the Danes. At some stage, as the coffin bearers went from Lindisfarne, they reached Norham [74:896477], whose Norman church by the river Tweed stands on the site of an older church which probably served a Christian community known to the Lindisfarne monks. It could be that from there they set out to travel by water to take shelter at Melrose; and that may account for the chapel and farm of St Cuthberts [74:871425] a little to the south of Norham.

Elsdon

They had to move on. The Danes entered Northumbria and the Borders, and so the coffin was carried south to Elsdon [80:936933] by a highway that goes across the Cheviots to the east of Dere Street. The church remembers the saint in its dedication. The journey on to the west took the sad party of monks across land that is now covered by Kielder Forest to Bewcastle [86:566747] to the north of Hadrian's Wall, where the Romans built and manned a fort in AD 120. The most striking thing about this remote moorland village is its elaborately carved Anglo-Saxon cross, which may well have been erected in defiance of the pagan Danes. It stands beside the St Cuthbert church, and the ruins of a thirteenth-century castle.

Scholars have calculated that this four-sided, 20-foot monolith was erected by Aldfrith around 690 in memory of a certain Alchfrith of Devra and his wife Gyneburh. On one of its sides it shows the figure of St John with the holy lamb; above that is a representation of Christ, and then at the foot there is a man with a hawk at his wrist. The other sides are covered with decorative figures of birds and animals, Anglian scrolls, knotwork and a tangle of runes, some of which have been attributed to Caedmon, the cowherd poet of Hilda's Whitby, but I find that rather fanciful.

In 883, Cuthbert's body was moved again, to be taken south from Chester-le-Street to Ripon, where it stayed until 995, when the monks were forced to flee before another wave of marauding Danes. They finally destroyed Wilfred's noble church, and wiped out the monastery that Eata had founded and which Cuthbert knew as a young man.

The story goes that for three weeks the monks carried their burden northeast from there. Perhaps they had in mind to seek shelter across the wall again, but when they came to Ward-Lawe to the east of Durham, a city which still had to come into existence, they found they could not move the coffin. It was as though it had been bolted to the ground. So for three days they fasted and prayed to be told what they should do next. They were given the answer that they should go to Dunholme or Durham, but naturally they had no idea where that was. As long as they were actively seeking that place, however, the coffin allowed itself to be carried.

One day as they journeyed they heard one woman complain to another that she had lost her cow. The other replied that the creature had been seen at Dunholme, and so by following the cow's owner they were able to discover the place they had been looking for. Once again an animal had come to Cuddy's aid. The next year they started to build a stone cathedral over the tomb in which the coffin was laid. Perhaps in honour of Ninian's Candida Casa, it became known as the White House.

The White House of Durham was completed in 1017. By the end of the century it was demolished and Cuthbert's body was moved again, but this time it did not travel far. On 11 August 1093, during the rule of Bishop St Carileph, work was started on the massive cathedral we know today. No one can tell for certain where the Saxon building which first housed the saint's tomb stood; but it is known that in 1104 his coffin, which had lain in the close of the new cathedral, was moved to its present position behind the high altar.

When Cuthbert's body was moved, it was given out that it was still untouched by decay. That was the sort of mystery that was often spoken of in order to bring pilgrims to a particular place and so draw money to a religious foundation and the city around it. In this case it was surely hardly necessary to tell of miracles. Cuthbert was the people's saint as he had been their bishop, and whether he was in the flesh or out of it they flocked to him, and their devotion earned them special dispensations. The Bolden Book of Durham transcribed in 1183 mentions the Haliwerfolk. These people were men of the Palatinate, who held their lands by virtue of the protection they afforded the saint's body, and who were not forced against their will to cross the Tyne or Tees in defence of the kingdom at large.

The Culdees

The story of the northern Celtic Church ends where it began, with the vanished Picts. Those who would follow the tale to its close must travel to Scotland's northeast.

When the Church in Britain accepted the Roman form of administration at the Synod of Whitby, the Picts continued to observe the rites of the Celtic Church. Many priests kept to the Druidic tonsure, and calculated Easter by the old tables. In these and other more pervasive ways they preserved the form of Christianity which they had learned from Columba. To try to understand the organization of the Church after Whitby, it is necessary to take a further look at the few pieces of evidence that the Picts left behind them.

In the twelfth century, an Icelandic writer described the Picts as small men who did wonders in the mornings and the evenings but who lost their strength at midday and went underground. Perhaps that was a reference to the elaborate, well-paved and completely mysterious underground passages that are associated with their culture.

One of the best examples of such a passage is to be seen at Tealing on the A929 between Forfar and Dundee. This passage, which was made in the first or second century, is to the east of the main road. You reach it by walking along a farm road until you come to a woodland path following the course of a stream. Part of the slab-stoned passageway is roofed, but it is the elaborately carved spirals of the cup and ring marks on the entrance stones that will take your attention. Who knows when this passage was last used and for what purpose? After all, what did the Picts who upheld the form of Christianity they had been taught by Ninian and Columba make of this remnant of their pagan past?

At least that passage and its inscribed stones confirm one of the few things we know for certain about this lost people. The Picts were cunning craftsmen, as the early hoard of silverware which was discovered on St Ninian's Isle in Shetland has proved, and as the long continuance of silver-smithing in the town of Inverness, which they founded, bears witness.

The Carved Stones

Yet it is the carved stones, some of which date from as late as the ninth century, which have the most to tell us about this vanished people. On these stones the ikons of the Christian faith of the Picts and the hunting and battle scenes of their secular lives are combined with the ornate and intricate decorations which they inherited from their pagan forebears, and which continue to puzzle scholars. Three of these carved stones stand on the roadside in Angus by the village of Aberlemno between Forfar and Brechin. Another stands in the churchyard of that village. There is a lively sophistication about the carvings on all these four stones; the realism with which the men in the hunting scenes are portrayed and the vitality of their animals make a vivid contrast to the stiff symbolism of the angels (which the Pictish scholar Isobel Henderson has likened to the figures in the Columban Book of Kells) and the angular formality of the biblical figures which flank the simple crosses.

The most puzzling thing about the Pictish stones is the curious recurring symbols with which they are decorated. These motifs include a Z-shaped rod, a hieroglyph that looks like a mirror and a comb, and a long-snouted swimming beast somewhat resembling an elephant except that his slender trunk grows between his ears.

Collections of the stones can be seen at St Vigeans on the A92 to the north of Arbroath, and at Meigle on the A94 to the northeast of Coupar Angus. One of the eighth-century stones in the Meigle collection shows the Celtic horned god Cernunnos, suggesting that it was often possible for paganism and Christianity to exist side by side. That is also borne out by a story that is associated with Meigle village itself, which lies in the shadow of the Sidlaw Hills. One of the nine daughters of the eighth-century St Donald of Ogilvy is supposed to have settled here, and danced with her sisters in the oakwoods, hoping to produce visions of their future husbands.

Monymusk

To the north of Meigle is the model village of Monymusk, between the A944 and the A96 to the west of Aberdeen. Its connection with the Columban Church is that it long housed the reliquary of the saint, which was taken to the Battle of Bannockburn, together with St Fillan's relics.

It is difficult to associate this nineteenth-century estate village with any such romantic and bloodthirsty pageantry. Monymusk is built round a square, quite unlike the usual Scottish street village, and the only immediate sign of the remote past is the twelfth-century Romanesque church which once housed the reliquary. That treasure is now in the National Museum of Antiquities in Edinburgh, but the church contains an unhewn, 7-foot-high granite boulder which was found on a nearby farm. The stone is marked with an equal-armed Celtic cross, and probably dates from the ninth century. The mark of the cross is engraved above Pictish symbols, one of which is thought to represent a casket and to have been drawn by somebody who was aware of the Columban reliquary.

Long before the relic of Columba was venerated at Monymusk the serious attacks on the Church he founded were under way. They began when Nectan, who became king of the Picts in 706, declared his allegiance to Rome. He aimed to throw out all the adherents to the old regime and to expel the monks who remained loyal to the Celtic order. When his reign was four years old, he caused a stone church to be built in the Saxon style at Restenneth to the west of Forfar. The site of that church, which is reached by a lane running off the B9113, is now occupied by a building which dates for the most part from the time of the medieval Augustinian monastery which was set up here. However, the tower retains evidence of two periods of Saxon work one of which could have originated with Nectan.

Curitan (Boniface)

The king was helped in his work of Romanizing the Celtic Church by Curitan (better known perhaps as Boniface). He was a Celtic priest, ardent for the practices of Rome, who travelled widely throughout the country. According to Bede, his labours resulted in a Scotland where the nation corrected rejoiced that it has been devoted as it were to a new discipleship of Peter, the most blessed Prince of the Apostles, and placed under the protection of his patronage' (Bede, Book V, ch. xxi; translated by A. O. Anderson.)

The mentioned of Peter refers both to the influence of Rome and to the number of churches at this time which were dedicated to the apostle. Throughout the land churches, such as St Moluag's cell at Rosemarkie, lost the name of their founders and were handed over to the patronage of Peter. By the mid-eighth century, the churches on the ancient Pictish sites of Tealing and Meigle had Peter churches. Ardent as Curitan was for the Roman ways, the very extent of his travels proves that he retained the Celtic love of wandering. There are even a few places where he settled which bear his own name in the Celtic manner. One such, Cladh Churidain, 'Curitan's settlement', is at Corrimony in Glen Urquhart, in the woods to the southwest of the chambered cairn [26:375299]; while his croft and well are in the hills to the north by Buntait [26:396309].

By 715 Nectan's 'reforms' were almost complete. He had imposed the Roman Easter throughout Pictland, and two years later the Church of Iona was expelled for refusing to conform to that usage. Meanwhile Nectan had thrown the Columbans out of the monastery in the old Pictish capital of Abernethy and established his own political and religious centre at Scone. After Nectan's death the primacy reverted to Abernethy for a hundred years until Kenneth mac Alpin, who united the Scots of Dalriada with the Picts of the east, established the capital for the whole country at Dunkeld.

Abernethy

The church of Abernethy (on the A913 to the west of Newburgh on the Firth of Tay) stands on a site that was a Christian place of worship from 460. The original church was restored by Columba's followers in 590 with the blessing of Gartnaidh, king of both northern and southern Picts. It was dedicated to Bride, that most Celtic of all female saints, and although the building was replaced the people who worshipped there remained faithful to the Irish usage until 1272.

The most startling thing about Abernethy today is the Irish round tower which stands beside the church. Whether it was built in the eighth or the ninth century (and the date of its construction is still questioned), it is certainly the most ancient complete monument in the whole of Scotland. In common with all such towers, which were partly used for defence, the doorway, which is set in the north side, is placed a few feet up in the wall.

It was in the shadow of this tower that the Pictish Christians who could not accept the decisions of the Synod of Whitby kept their own form of Celtic Christianity alive until they were finally broken in the thirteenth century. To understand the spirit which urged them on in this long-standing defiance of Rome, we have to try to disentangle the emotions behind the issue. The immediate and much rehearsed bones of contention concerning the date on which Easter was to be kept, the style of the tonsure, and whether or not the washing of feet should be part of Church ritual simply cannot account for the bitter heart-searchings and searing divisions that went on in the early Church. Nora Chadwick, a great Celtic scholar, has explained in *The Age of the Saints in the Early Celtic Church* that basically the struggle was between a Church which reflected an urban civilization 'based on ancient legal and administrative precedent' where 'the bishop had his see, his *sedes* in the cities which were the the ancient administrative centres of the province', and a Church inspired during the fourth and fifth centuries by the mysticism of the solitary hermits whom we know as the Desert Fathers, and whose adherents lived in small, isolated rural communities. The latter form of organization, in which the bishop had a lesser administrative role than the abbot of the community, would obviously be best suited to the autonomy of the communities of Christians who lived their lives away from the centres of government. It would be a hard and painful decision for such a Church to relinquish its autonomy.

The keeping of Easter by the old calculation which linked the observance of the Christian festival more firmly to the Hebrew Passover was an obvious way in which the Celtic Church could retain its identity. On Lindisfarne, Aidan managed to observe the Celtic Easter until his death in 651; and although Adomnan tried (albeit unsuccessfully) to persuade the Church in the north of Ireland to change to the Roman Easter, he was rebuked by Ceolfrid, abbot of Jarrow, for keeping his Celtic tonsure. The conversion of the Celtic Church to Roman usage in Northumbria was largely the responsibility of two people whose backgrounds lay in the old teaching but who had little else in common. One was Hilda, abbess of the double monastery at Whitby; the other was Wilfrid, who founded the Benedictine monastery at Ripon.

Hilda

Hilda, who was born in 614, was related to the royal families of both Northumberland and East Anglia. She was baptized by Paulinus and, when she was thirty-three, Aidan gave her a plot of land on the north bank of the Wear in order that she might start a religious foundation. From there she moved to become abbess of Hartlepool, and ten years later she founded her own double monastery at Whitby. This foundation was to become famous for its scholarship, and for housing Caedmon, the cowherd poet, to whom the Anglo-Saxon 'Hymn of the Creation' is attributed. Six years after its inception, Whitby was to host the synod which was to decide the form of British Christianity until the Reformation; and Hilda herself, who had previously been an advocate of the Celtic Church, conformed to its decision. Yet she retained one trait characteristic of the Celtic saints, a peculiar affinity with birds. Wild geese would stop at Whitby on their migratory flights to and from the Arctic to pay homage to her.

Wilfrid

Wilfrid was a completely different personality. The son of a noble family, he was born about the same time as Cuthbert and educated at Lindisfarne. His ambitions were worldly and urbane, and he soon felt irked by the limitations of the island sanctuary, so at the age of twenty he got Aidan's permission to go to Canterbury. From there he journeyed to Rome. It was then that he discovered a natural affinity with Roman ritual, so when he returned to England to take up his position as abbot of Ripon he introduced a Benedictine rule and kept Easter according to Roman usage.

After his victory at the Synod of Whitby, at which he was the chief champion of Rome, he spent some months in France being consecrated as a bishop of York by twelve French bishops at Compiègne, there being a lack of British bishops of sufficient standing to undertake that task. Not surprisingly he was little loved by the people at home, and his proud power gained him the jealous enmity of the leaders of both Church and State. Yet throughout his long, uneasy life he managed to amass wealth, obtaining large endowments of land for his churches, and building the costly church and monastery at Hexham. He died far to the south, at Oundle in Northamptonshire.

He was seventy-six and retained his worldly wisdom to the end, bequeathing some of his massive fortune to his abbots so that they could buy the friendship of kings and bishops.

The decision at Whitby left the Church torn between rival factions, and that would have been so whatever the outcome. The Pictish Church was deeply involved in the disputes which rent Northumbria; and it was the Pictish bishop Trumwine who was one of the first mediators between the opposing factions. As we have seen, he was responsible for asking Cuthbert to accept the role of bishop and use his kindness and good sense to heal the bitterness that was dividing the Church.

Colman

Both Trumwine and Cuthbert were unable to reconcile Colman, who succeeded Aidan and Finan as abbot of Lindisfarne, to the new regime. He had been the chief defender of the Celtic Church at Whitby and found it quite impossible to accept the decision of the synod, so with thirty of his monks he left Northumberland for Iona. Finally, as that sanctuary became threatened by Roman dominion, he crossed the sea to Ireland and founded his own monastery in County Galway on the Isle of Inishbofin.

It was dissidents such as Colman who were the inspiration of the Culdee Church, which managed to persist in the east of Scotland throughout the eighth and ninth centuries.

In the east window of the church at Monymusk a piece of modern stained glass shows a Culdee priest, dressed in his white alb, preaching to three women, two soldiers and two sheep. The artist probably had in mind one of the latter Culdees who maintained the church here throughout the Dark Ages, as they did at Abernethy, Brechin and Dunkeld. Perhaps he was thinking of one of the religious trained on the island sanctuary in Loch Leven, to the south of Abernethy, where St Servanus (sometimes confused with Kentigern's teacher, St Serf of Culross) lived for seven years with his Culdees at the end of the seventh century. The Culdee community continued there until the twelfth century, and these priests were so generally accepted in the north that up to 936 they officiated at St Peter's in York, where the canons were referred to as Culdees until the reign of Henry II.

The word 'Culdee' (*Ceile de*) simply means servant of God. The term was first used in Ireland to describe a religious recluse who gave himself wholly to the service of God, although, unlike a monk, he was still able to retain private property. For some reason the Culdees were tolerated by Nectan, perhaps because their organization was fairly fluid. So when the Columban Church was banned in the east, the Culdees still gave a distinctive character to northern Christianity.

During the eighth and ninth centuries, the Picts gradually gained control of the whole of Scotland, and finally so merged their identity in the nation that they lost it for ever. In the early ninth century the country was still divided, although it all seems to have been under Pictish control. From 789 to 820, Constantine reigned in the east, while his son Donald, who predeceased him by nine years, was king in Dalriada. It was Constantine who took control of the northern churches away from Iona and gave it to Dunkeld.

Dunkeld

The central position of that city, just north of Perth, makes it the natural choice for an administrative capital; so it is understandable that it should have had this religious significance even before Kenneth mac Alpin chose it for his seat of government. Convenience was not the only matter at stake. At a deeper level, the change of focus from Iona to Dunkeld fitted in with the change of Church organization from one suited to isolated rural communities to a form that had been evolved for city dwellers.

Kenneth appointed a bishop to Dunkeld, and to strengthen the city's religious power and, perhaps, to appease the loyal adherents to the Celtic Church, he is said to have brought relics of Columba from Iona to the new cathedral. His excuse was that they would be safer on the mainland, and less vulnerable to attacks from Danish raiders than on the tiny undefended island.

Brechin

The other cathedral served by the Culdees was at Brechin to the northeast of Aberdeen. The present medieval cathedral there is flanked by an Irish round tower of the tenth century, which rivals the one at Abernethy. Brechin's tower is 86 feet high, and is crowned by an octagonal cap which raises it another 20 feet. Its walls are 3½ feet thick at the base, and its internal diameter remains at a constant 8 feet throughout its seven storeys. In the usual manner of such towers, its entrance is about 6 feet above ground level.

Despite the official dominance of Dunkeld and Brechin, Iona remained a goal for pilgrimage for several centuries. In the tenth century, the Irish-Norse king of Dublin joined the throng of pilgrims travelling to the island that his countrymen had ravaged. Did he pause, I wonder, on the silver sands that edge the translucent green sea of Martyr's Bay, where his eighth-century countrymen had slaughtered the monks?

Irish pilgrims continued to come to Iona for another two thousand years, but by the late Middle Ages the island was almost as deserted as Columba had prophesied. By the time that Dr Johnson and Boswell arrived here, the only lodging they could find was in a derelict barn beside the ruins of the medieval abbey and nunnery. At least they felt that they were on sacred ground and were moved by the religious memories that the place held. Such impulses did not noticeably stir Queen Victoria; she did not even bother to land on Iona when she cruised past the island.

The Iona that the twelfth-century pilgrims came to was an established part of the Roman Church. It was secured in that position by the work of St Margaret, the eleventh-century English queen of the savage and bloodthirsty Malcolm, who terrorized both Northumbria and Cumbria until he was killed by treachery at Alnwick. A total contrast to her husband, Margaret would rather have been a nun than a queen, and her humility was such that she astounded her courtiers by kneeling to wash the feet of a beggar. Dissatisfied with the state of the Church in Scotland, she argued for a celibate priesthood and for an extension of the Benedictine rule. Her own personal acts of piety were to build the church at Dunfermline, to restore the abbey on Iona, and to encourage pilgrims from Lothian to visit St Andrews by establishing a ferry between the south and north shores of the Firth of Forth.

With Margaret, the Celtic Church in Scotland came to an end, and gradually the Culdees were replaced by a priesthood that was more acceptable to Rome. The story was much the same throughout the whole of Britain. In Wales, the Celtic Church maintained its independence from Rome for nearly a century after the edicts of the Synod of Whitby; and in Devon and Cornwall Celts retained their autonomy until the tenth century.

As long as the Celtic Church lasted, the impulse to travel continued. There is a record in the Anglo-Saxon Chronicle for 891 of three Irishmen who came to Cornwall in a coracle made of two and a half hides. They had set out 'because they wished for the love of God to be on pilgrimage, they cared not where' (*Parker Chronicle*, translated and edited by G. N. Garmonsway, Dent, 1953).

Bibliography

J. Romully Allen, *The Early Christian Monuments of Scotland*, Society of Antiquaries of Scotland, 1903

A. O. Anderson (ed.), *Early Sources of Scottish History AD 500–1286*, Oliver & Boyd, 1922

M. O. Anderson, *Kings and Kingships in Early Scotland*, Scottish Academic Press, 1973

Kate Y. A. Bone, *St Kentigern*, OUP, 1948

Gerald Bonner, 'St Cuthbert and the Hiberno-Northern Tradition', Lecture to the Joint Anglican Orthodox Pilgrimage to Lindisfarne, 1983

Gerald Bonner, 'The Holy Spirit Within – St Cuthbert as a Western Orthodox Saint', *Sobernost*, vol. 1, no. 1, 1979

J. Bullock, *The Life of the Celtic Church*, St Andrew Press, 1963

Marian Campbell, *Argyll, the Enduring Heartland*, Turnstone Press, 1977

Alexander Carmichael, *Carmina Gaedelica*, Oliver & Boyd, 1954

Nora K. Chadwick, *The Age of the Saints in the Early Celtic Church: Lectures delivered at the University of Durham*, OUP, 1961

Betram Colgrave, *Two Lives of St Cuthbert*, CUP, 1940

Hilda Colgrave, *St Cuthbert of Durham*, Northumberland Press, 1947

Rosemary Cramp, *The Background to St Cuthbert's Life*, Durham Cathedral Lecture, 1980

Ian Finlay, *Columba*, Gollancz, 1979

Leslie Hardinge, *The Celtic Church in Britain*, SPCK, 1972

I. Henderson, *The Picts*, Thames & Hudson, 1951

Kathleen Herbert, *The Lady of the Fountain*, Bran's Head, Frome, 1982 (a novel based on the life of Kentigern's mother)

Rosalind Hill, 'Christianity and Geography in Early Northumbria', *Studies in Church History*, vol. III, ed. G. J. Cuming, CUP, 1972

Diana Leatham, *Celtic Sunrise*, Hodder & Stoughton, 1951

Diana Leatham, *They Built on Rock*, Celtic Art Society, 1948

Joseph Barber Lightfoot, *Leaders of the Northern Church*, Macmillan, 1890

Lorn Macintyre, 'The Secrets of Hinba', *Scots Magazine*, June 1983

A. C. McKerracher, 'The Dewars of St Fillan', *Scots Magazine*, January 1984

G. R. D. McLean, *Poems of the Western Highlands*, SPCK, 1961

F. Marian McNeill, *Iona, a History of the Land*, Blackie, 1973

Eona K. McNicholl, *Lamp in the Night Wind*, Maclellan, 1965 (a novel based on the life of Columba on Iona)

J. MacQueen, *St Nynia*, Oliver & Boyd, 1961

Arthur Murray, *St Columba and the Holy Isle of the Garvellachs*, Oliver & Boyd, 1980

W. Douglas Simpson, *St Ninian and the Origins of the Celtic Church in Scotland*, Oliver & Boyd, 1940

W. Douglas Simpson, *The Celtic Church in Scotland*, Aberdeen University Press, 1935

W. Douglas Simpson, *The Historical Columba*, Hutchinson, 1927

Charles Thomas, *The Early Christian Archaeology of North Britain*, OUP, 1971

Index